Go Programming for Beginners

Master Go from Scratch with Easy-to-Follow Step

Tommy Clark

Disclaimer

The information provided in *"Go Programming for Beginners: Master Go from Scratch with Easy-to-Follow Steps"* by **Tommy Clark** is intended solely for educational and informational purposes. While every effort has been made to ensure the accuracy and completeness of the content, the author and publisher make no guarantees regarding the results that may be achieved by following the instructions or techniques described in this book.

Readers are encouraged to seek appropriate professional guidance for specific issues or challenges they may encounter, particularly in commercial or critical environments.

The author and publisher disclaim all liability for any loss, damage, or inconvenience arising directly or indirectly from the use or misuse of the information contained within this book. Any reliance on the information provided is at the reader's own risk.

Introduction

Welcome to **"Go Programming for Beginners: Master Go from Scratch with Easy-to-Follow Steps."** Programming languages that are reliable, effective, and scalable are more important than ever in the rapidly changing world of technology. Google developed Go, often called Golang, to meet these demands, and because of its ease of use and speed, it has swiftly gained popularity among developers.

This book is suited for anyone starting out in programming or looking to broaden their skill set using a language that is becoming more and more popular across a variety of industries.

We will unlock the potential of the Go programming language in this thorough book, which will break it down into simple ideas and useful examples. No prior knowledge of coding is required; we begin at the very beginning and walk you through all of Go's subtleties step-by-step. Every chapter builds on the one before it, assisting you in becoming more competent and self-assured.

As you read this book, you will discover:

the basic ideas of programming and how Go makes everyday chores easier.

How to rapidly get started by configuring your programming environment.

Variables, control structures, functions, and error handling are examples of fundamental language elements.

the distinctive concurrent programming concepts of Go.

The best methods for writing that are clear, effective, and readable Go ahead and write code.

projects and real-world applications to solidify your understanding.

The skills you acquire here will give you a solid basis for your future pursuits, whether your objective is to create online applications, cloud services, or system-level programming.

You are urged to actively interact with the content. Take the time to comprehend the ideas being taught, try out the examples, and play around with the code. In addition to learning how to write Go code, you will also acquire a problem-solving mindset that is essential for any programming endeavor as you work through the chapters.

Chapter 1: Getting Started with Go

Greetings from the Go universe! Go, an open-source programming language developed at Google in 2007, is also referred to as Golang. Its design prioritized productivity, efficiency, and simplicity. This chapter will provide the groundwork for you to grasp Go's essential features, set up your development environment, and write your first Go program as you start your road to become an expert.

Why Opt for Go?

Understanding the reasons for Go's rise in popularity among developers is crucial before delving into the practical elements. Here are some strong arguments:

Simplicity and Clarity: Go is easy to understand and write because of its clear syntax. By removing clutter and intricate features that are frequently present in other languages, it frees engineers to concentrate on problem-solving rather than juggling linguistic nuances.

Concurrency Support: Go is well known for its strong concurrent programming capabilities. By utilizing the capabilities of contemporary multi-core CPUs, Go's goroutines and channels facilitate the management of several tasks concurrently.

Performance: Go is made to move quickly. Because Go is built, programs written in it can run as fast as those written in C or C++ while still offering features like garbage collection and robust typing.

The Go standard library, which includes packages for everything from HTTP servers to cryptography, is robust and extensive. This implies that you can frequently do activities without the need for third-party libraries by utilizing built-in characteristics.

Excellent Tooling: Go has a strong toolchain that makes formatting, testing, and dependency management easier. Essential tools for Go development include `go fmt`, `go test`, and `go get`.

Setting Up Your Development Environment

Before we can start writing Go code, we need to ensure we have the right environment setup. Follow thesesteps to get started:

1. Install Go

To install Go, follow these steps:

Download: Visit the official Go website at golang.org/dl and download the appropriate version for your operating system (Windows, macOS, Linux).

Install: Follow the installation instructions provided for your OS. On Windows, this typically involves running an installer; on macOS and Linux, you might need to use a package manager or extract the archive.

Verify Installation: Open a terminal or command prompt and run the command:
```

go version
```

This should display the installed version of Go.

2. Set Up Workspace

Go utilizes a workspace that organizes your code. Traditionally, the workspace is defined in a directory with a specific structure. You can set up your workspace by following these steps:

Create a Directory: Create a directory where you will keep your Go projects. The convention is to place this under a directory named `go` in your home directory, but you can adjust this based on your preference.
```

mkdir ~/go
```

Set GOPATH: Set the `GOPATH` environment variable to point to your newly created directory. This helps Go locate your projects and dependencies.

- For Unix/Linux or macOS, add the following line to your `~/.bashrc` or `~/.zshrc`:
```bash
export GOPATH=~/go
export PATH=$PATH:$GOPATH/bin
```

```
```

- For Windows, you can set the environment variable via the System Properties or using PowerShell:
```powershell
$env:GOPATH='C:\path\to\your\go'
```

Create Directories: Inside your `GOPATH`, create a directory for the source code:
```
mkdir -p ~/go/src
```

3. Choose an Editor

While you can write Go code in any text editor, using an IDE or code editor that has good Go integration will enhance your productivity. Popular editors for Go development include:

VS Code: Lightweight and customizable with a plethora of extensions for Go.
GoLand: A powerful IDE from JetBrains, focused entirely on Go development.

Atom: Another customizable editor with Go packages.

Sublime Text: A popular code editor with Go support via plugins.

4. Write Your First Program

Now that your environment is set up, it's time to write your first Go program! Open your text editor and create a new file named `hello.go` in your `~/go/src` directory. Add the following code:

```go
package main
import "fmt" func main() {
fmt.Println("Hello, World!")
}
```

5. Run Your Program

To run your newly created program, follow these steps:

Open your terminal and navigate to the directory where you saved `hello.go`:
```bash
cd ~/go/src
```

Run the program using the Go command:
```bash
go run hello.go
```

You should see the output:
```

Hello, World!
```

As we move forward in this book, we'll delve deeper into Go's features, explore advanced concepts, and build real-world applications. The journey truly is just beginning, and the next chapter will take us into thefundamentals of Go programming, where you'll learn about variables, control structures, and basic data types. Let's keep building our Go knowledge together!

Setting Up Your Go Environment

The Go programming language, also known as Golang, has gained immense popularity due to its simplicity, speed, and efficiency in handling concurrent tasks. Whether you're a seasoned developer or a newcomer to the world of programming, setting up your Go environment correctly is crucial for a smooth development experience. This chapter will guide you through the necessary steps to get your Go environment up and running, ensuring you have everything you need to start building robust applications.

1. Why Go?

Before diving into the setup process, it's worth understanding why you might want to use Go. Created by Google engineers Robert Griesemer, Rob Pike, and Ken Thompson, Go is designed with simplicity and efficiency in mind. Its features include:

Concurrency: Go's goroutines and channels make it easy to write concurrent code.
Performance: Go is a compiled language, which

means it's close to the metal and provides fast execution times.
Simplicity and Readability: Go syntax is clean and minimalistic, making it easier to read and maintain code.
Rich Standard Library: Go comes with a powerful standard library that supports a wide range of functionalities out of the box.

With these advantages in mind, let's get started on setting up your Go environment.## 2. Prerequisites
Before you install Go, ensure that you have the following:

A modern operating system: Go is compatible with Windows, macOS, and Linux.
An internet connection: You'll need to download the Go installer and any dependencies.## 3. Downloading Go
3.1. Official Go Installation

Visit the official Go website: Go to golang.org/dl to download the latest version of Go.

Choose the correct installer: Select the installer that matches your operating system:
Windows: `.msi` installer
macOS: `.pkg` installer
Linux: A `.tar.gz` archive

Download the file: Click the download link and save the file to your computer.### 3.2. Installing Go
Windows: Double-click the downloaded `.msi` file and follow the installation wizard. By default, it installs Go in `C:\Go`.

macOS: Open the downloaded `.pkg` file and follow the installation steps. Go will typically be installed in `/usr/local/go`.

Linux: Use the command line to extract the archive. For example:

```bash
wget https://golang.org/dl/go<VERSION>.linux-amd64.tar.gz sudo tar -C /usr/local -xzf go<VERSION>.linux-amd64.tar.gz
```

Replace `<VERSION>` with the actual version number you downloaded.## 4. Setting Up Environment Variables After installation, you need to set up your environment variables. This is essential for Go to run correctly.### 4.1. Setting `GOPATH` and `PATH`
GOPATH: This is the location of your workspace, where your Go projects will reside. By default, it's set to `~/go` on Linux and macOS, and `%USERPROFILE%\go` on Windows. You can customize this, but it's common to leave it as is.

PATH: You need to add the Go binary directory to your `PATH` to easily run Go commands from any terminal.

For each operating system, here's how to set these variables:

Windows:

Search for "Environment Variables" in the Start menu and select "Edit the system environment variables".
In the System Properties window, click on "Environment Variables".
Under "User variables," click "New" to create a `GOPATH` variable and set its value to `%USERPROFILE%\go`.
Find the "Path" variable, select it, and click "Edit". Add the following paths:
`C:\Go\bin`
`%USERPROFILE%\go\bin`

macOS/Linux:
Open your shell configuration file (e.g., `.bashrc`, `.bash_profile`, or `.zshrc`) and add the following lines:

```bash
export GOPATH=$HOME/go
export PATH=$PATH:/usr/local/go/bin:$GOPATH/bin
```

Then, run `source ~/.bashrc` (or the appropriate file name) to apply the changes. ## 5. Verifying Your Installation
To ensure that Go is correctly installed, you can run the following command in your terminal or commandprompt:

```bash
go version
```

This should return the installed version of Go, confirming that the setup was successful.## 6. Creating Your First Go

Project
With your Go environment set up, it's time to create your
first Go project:

Open your terminal (or command prompt).
Navigate to your workspace by running:

```bash
cd $GOPATH/src
```

Create a new directory for your project:

```bash
mkdir hello-worldcd hello-world
```

Create a new file named `main.go`:

```bash
touch main.go
```

Open `main.go` in your favorite text editor and add the
following code:

```go
package mainimport "fmt"
func main() { fmt.Println("Hello, World!")
}
```

Finally, run your Go application by executing:

```bash
go run main.go
```

You should see `Hello, World!` displayed in your terminal.

The next chapters will dive deeper into Go's syntax, features, and best practices, helping you to become a proficient Go developer. Remember, the key to mastering any programming language is practice and persistence — so keep coding!

Go Programming Fundamentals

Go, often referred to as Golang, is a statically typed, compiled programming language designed for simplicity and efficiency, developed by Google in 2009. Its design aims to combine the ease of programming with the performance and security of a systems-level language. In this chapter, we will delve into the fundamental aspects of Go, covering its syntax, core concepts, and unique features that make it a compelling choice for developers.

1. Setting Up Go Environment

Before you start coding in Go, you need to set up your development environment:### Installing Go
Download Go: Visit the official Go programming language website (https://golang.org) and download the installer for your operating system.
Install Go: Run the installer and follow the on-screen

instructions.

Set GOPATH: Go uses an environment variable called GOPATH to specify the location of your workspace. It typically defaults to a directory named `go` in your home directory.

Verify Installation: Open your terminal or command prompt and run `go version`. If the installation is successful, you will see the installed version of Go.

Setting Up Your Workspace

Go follows a specific folder structure for organizing code. Create a directory for your Go projects (commonly called `workspace`) and create subdirectories for your Go applications within it. Your workspaceshould look like:

```
$HOME/gobin/
pkg/src/
your_project/main.go
```

2. Basic Syntax and Structure### Hello, World! in Go
Every programming journey begins with printing "Hello, World!" to the console. Below is a simple Goprogram:

```go
package main
import "fmt" func main() {
fmt.Println("Hello, World!")
```

```
}
```

Package Declaration: Every Go program starts with a package declaration. The `main` package is special because it defines the entry point of the executable application.
Import Statement: The `import` keyword allows you to include other packages. The standard library package `fmt` is used here for formatting and output.
Function Declaration: The `main` function is where execution begins. It has to be defined for any executable Go program.

Comments

You can add comments in Go using `//` for single-line comments or `/* ... */` for multi-line comments.

```go
// This is a single-line comment

/*
This is a
multi-line comment
*/
```

3. Variables and Data Types### Declaring Variables
In Go, you can declare variables using the `var` keyword or short declaration syntax with `:=`.

```go
```

```go
var a int = 10 // Using var
b := 20        // Short declaration for intfmt.Println(a, b)
```

Basic Data Types

Go has several built-in data types:

Integer Types: `int`, `int8`, `int16`, `int32`, `int64`
Unsigned Integer Types: `uint`, `uint8`, `uint16`, `uint32`, `uint64`
Floating Point Types: `float32`, `float64`
Boolean Type: `bool`
String Type: `string`### Constants
Constants in Go can be declared using the `const` keyword and are immutable.

```go
const pi = 3.14
```

4. Control Structures

Conditional Statements

Go supports the traditional `if`, `else if`, and `else` conditional statements.

```go
if a < b {
fmt.Println("a is less than b")
} else if a == b { fmt.Println("a is equal to b")
} else {
```

```go
fmt.Println("a is greater than b")
}
```

Switch Statement

The `switch` statement is an alternative to long `if-else` chains.

```go
switch day := 3; day {case 1:
fmt.Println("Monday")case 2:
fmt.Println("Tuesday")case 3:
fmt.Println("Wednesday")default:
fmt.Println("Another day")
}
```

Loops

Go provides a single looping construct, the `for` loop, which can be used in several ways:

```go
// Classic for loop
for i := 0; i < 5; i++ {fmt.Println(i)
}

// For each loop with rangeslice := []int{1, 2, 3, 4, 5}
for index, value := range slice {fmt.Println(index, value)
}
```

5. Functions

Functions in Go are defined using the `func` keyword. Go supports multiple return values, which is a powerful feature.

```go
func add(a int, b int) (int, error) {return a + b, nil
}

result, err := add(3, 5)
```

Defer Statements

The `defer` keyword allows you to postpone the execution of a function until the surrounding functionreturns.

```go
func main() {
defer fmt.Println("Executed last") fmt.Println("Executed first")
}
```

6. Structs and Interfaces### Structs
Structs are user-defined types that allow grouping of data.

```go
type Person struct {Name string
Age int
}
```

```go
p := Person{Name: "Alice", Age: 30} fmt.Println(p.Name,
p.Age)
```

Interfaces

Interfaces in Go enable polymorphism. They allow you to specify methods that must be implemented.

```go
type Animal interface {Speak() string
}

type Dog struct{}

func (d Dog) Speak() string {return "Woof!"
}

var a Animal = Dog{}fmt.Println(a.Speak())
```

7. Error Handling

Go promotes explicit error handling through multiple return values. Common practice is to return an errorvalue alongside results.

```go
func divide(a int, b int) (int, error) {if b == 0 {
return 0, fmt.Errorf("division by zero")
}
return a / b, nil
}
```

```
// Usage
result, err := divide(10, 0)if err != nil {
fmt.Println(err)
} else { fmt.Println(result)
}
```
```

In this chapter, we covered the fundamentals of Go programming, including its syntax, core concepts, and practical examples. Go's simplicity, efficiency, and built-in support for concurrency make it a powerful language for both beginners and experienced developers. As we proceed through this book, we will exploremore advanced features and practical applications, equipping you with the skills needed to build robust applications with Go.
```

Chapter 2: Understanding Go ProgrammingStructure

Go, often referred to as Golang, is a statically typed, compiled language designed for simplicity and efficiency in system-level programming. Created by Google engineers Robert Griesemer, Rob Pike, and Ken Thompson, it has attracted a dedicated user community due to its excellent support for concurrent programming, garbage collection features, and rich standard library. In this chapter, we will explore the fundamental structure of Go programming, including its syntax, packages, types, functions, and the overall architecture that makes Go unique.

2.1 The Anatomy of a Go Program

At its core, a Go program comprises packages, functions, and basic types. Understanding how these elements work together is essential to writing clear and effective Go code.

2.1.1 Packages

A Go program is organized into packages. A package is a collection of related Go files, and it serves as a namespace to avoid conflicts among identifiers (such as variable names, function names, etc.). The Go standard library is divided into many packages, each responsible for a specific functionality.

The first line of a Go source file specifies the package name using the `package` keyword:

```go
package main
```

The `main` package is special because it indicates that the program is executable. Any Go file that belongs to the `main` package must have a `main` function, which serves as the entry point of the program.

2.1.2 Importing Packages

To leverage external packages, we can import them at the beginning of our Go files using the `import` keyword. This allows us to utilize functions and types defined in other packages.

```go
import (
"fmt"
"math"
)
```

In the above import statement, we use the `fmt` package for formatted I/O operations and the `math` package for mathematical functions.

2.1.3 Functions

Functions in Go are defined using the `func` keyword, followed by the function name, parameters, return types, and the function body. Functions promote code reusability and improve readability. Here's a simple example:

```go
func add(a int, b int) int {return a + b
}
```

In this case, we define a function called `add`, which takes two integers as parameters and returns their sum.
2.1.4 Types
Go is a statically typed language, meaning the type of variable must be known at compile time. The basictypes in Go include:

Integer types (e.g., `int`, `int64`, `uint`)
Floating-point types (e.g., `float64`)
Boolean type (`bool`)
String type (`string`)

You can declare variables with the `var` keyword:

```go
var age int = 30
```

Alternatively, Go provides a shorthand method using the `:=` operator for variable declaration andinitialization:

```go
name := "Alice"
```

2.1.5 Control Structures

28

Go offers standard control structures like `if`, `for`, and `switch` to facilitate flow control in programs. The `if` statement works similarly to other languages:

```go
if age >= 18 {
fmt.Println("You are an adult.")
}
```

The `for` loop is the only loop construct in Go, and it can be used with various syntaxes, including traditional counting and range-based loops:

```go
for i := 0; i < 5; i++ {fmt.Println(i)
}

for index, value := range []string{"a", "b", "c"} {
fmt.Println(index, value)
}
```

2.1.6 Concurrency in Go

One of the standout features of Go is its built-in support for concurrent programming through goroutines and channels.

Goroutines are lightweight threads managed by the Go runtime. You can launch a new goroutine by using the `go` keyword:

```go
go func() {
fmt.Println("This is run concurrently.")
}()
```

Channels are the conduits that allow goroutines to communicate with each other, facilitating data transfer while ensuring synchronization. Here's how we can create and use a channel:

```go
ch := make(chan int)

go func() {
ch <- 42 // Send data to channel
}()

value := <-ch // Receive data from channel
fmt.Println(value)
```

2.2 Error Handling

Error handling in Go is explicit and straightforward. Go functions often return multiple values, including an error type. You check for errors right after calling the function:

```go
result, err := someFunction()if err != nil {
fmt.Println("Error occurred:", err)return
}
```

```
```

This approach encourages developers to handle errors immediately, leading to cleaner and more reliablecode.

Understanding the structure of Go programming lays a strong foundation for writing effective applications. Through its use of packages, simple syntax, strong type system, and built-in concurrency features, Go promotes a clear and efficient method for building robust programs. In the following chapters, we will delve deeper into these concepts and explore how to leverage them to tackle real-world programming challenges.

By mastering the fundamentals outlined in this chapter, you will be well-equipped to write Go programs that are not only functional but also elegant and efficient. Whether you're newcomers to programming or experienced developers transitioning to Go, the principles in this chapter form the backbone of effective Go development.

Basics of Go Syntax and Structure

Understanding the syntax and structure of Go is essential for both new and experienced programmers alike. This chapter will delve into the foundational elements of Go programming, covering its syntax, conventions, and overall structure.

1. Introduction to Go's Syntax

Go's syntax is designed to be clean and readable, making it accessible for beginners while maintaining the robustness needed for professional development. Like many programming languages, Go is case-sensitive, and keywords are written in lowercase. The basic building blocks include variables, constants, data types, functions, and control structures.

1.1. Variable Declaration

Variables in Go can be declared using the `var` keyword, followed by the variable name and type. Alternatively, Go supports a shorthand declaration using the `:=` operator, which infers the variable's type:

```go
var age int = 30 name := "John Doe"
```

In the example above, `age` is declared as an integer variable using the `var` keyword, while `name` is declared using the shorthand method which automatically determines its type as a string from the assignedvalue.

1.2. Constants

Constants are declared similarly to variables but use the `const` keyword. Constants are immutable after their declaration and cannot be modified:

```go
const pi = 3.14
```

Constants can also be defined as typed constants, which

helps in cases where you want to specify a typeexplicitly.

2. Data Types

Go is statically typed, meaning that variable types are known at compile time. It features several built-in data types:

Basic Types: Includes integers (`int`, `int8`, `int16`, `int32`, `int64`), floating-point numbers (`float32`, `float64`), strings, and booleans.
Composite Types: Arrays, slices, maps, structs, and channels are composite types in Go that allow you to construct complex data structures.

Example of declaring different data types:

```go
var height float32 = 5.9 var isStudent bool = true
days := []string{"Monday", "Tuesday", "Wednesday"}
```

3. Control Structures

Control structures dictate the flow of execution in programs. Go offers several standard control structures:
3.1. Conditional Statements
Conditional statements allow for branching logic. The `if`, `else if`, and `else` statements provide a straightforward way to evaluate conditions:

```go
if age < 18 { fmt.Println("Minor")
```

```go
} else if age >= 18 && age < 65 {fmt.Println("Adult")
} else { fmt.Println("Senior")
}
```

3.2. Switch Statements

The `switch` statement provides a way to execute different cases based on a particular value. It can be more elegant than multiple `if` statements:

```go
switch day := "Tuesday"; day {case "Monday":
fmt.Println("Start of the week!")case "Tuesday":
fmt.Println("Second day of the week!")default:
fmt.Println("Another day!")
}
```

3.3. Loops

Go has a single looping construct, the `for` loop, which can be used in three ways: traditional, range-based,and as a while loop:

```go
// Traditional for loopfor i := 0; i < 5; i++ {
fmt.Println(i)
}

// Range-based for loop
names := []string{"Alice", "Bob", "Charlie"}
```

```go
for i, name := range names { fmt.Printf("%d: %s\n", i,
name)
}
```

4. Functions

Functions are first-class citizens in Go. They can return
multiple values, which is a unique feature that sets Go
apart from many other languages:

```go
func add(x int, y int) (int, error) {return x + y, nil
}
```

The use of named return values can also simplify the
understanding of code:

```go
func divide(x, y float64) (result float64, err error) {if y ==
0 {
err = fmt.Errorf("division by zero")return
}
result = x / yreturn
}
```

5. Package Structure

Go organizes code into packages. A package is a collection
of Go files in the same directory that are compiled
together. The `main` package is special as it defines the

35

starting point of the program. For example:

```go
package main
import "fmt" func main() {
fmt.Println("Hello, World!")
}
```

In this example, the `main` function acts as the entry point for the program. It's good practice to encapsulate related functions into their packages, which promotes modular programming and better organization of code.

The syntax and structure of Go are designed with simplicity and clarity in mind. Whether it's variable declaration, data types, control structures, or functions, each component contributes to writing clean, efficient code. As you continue your journey in learning Go, mastering its syntax will become second nature,paving the way for building robust applications in a straightforward manner. In the next chapter, we'll explore more advanced features and functionalities that Go offers, particularly focused on concurrency and networking.

With this foundational understanding of Go's syntax and structure, you are well-equipped to start writing meaningful code in one of the most efficient programming languages available today. Let's dive deeper into what makes Go truly powerful!

Essential Building Blocks: Variables and Constants in Go

In the world of programming, understanding the basic building blocks of a language is crucial for both beginners and seasoned developers. Go, also known as Golang, is designed with simplicity and efficiency in mind. One of the fundamental elements that support this vision are variables and constants. This chapter will delve deep into these essential building blocks, exploring their definitions, usage, and best practices within the Go programming language.

1.1 Introduction to Variables### What is a Variable?
In programming, a variable is a storage location identified by a name that holds a value. This value can change during the execution of a program. Think of a variable as a labeled box in which you can place data. You can open the box (access the variable) and update its contents (change its value) whenever needed.

Declaring Variables in Go

Go provides several ways to declare variables, making it easy for both beginners and experienced developers. Here are the most common methods:

Using the `var` Keyword

The `var` keyword is the traditional way to declare a variable in Go. Here's the syntax:

```go
```

```
var variableName variableType
```

For example:

```go
var age int
```

This declares a variable `age` of type `int`, but it doesn't assign a value yet. You can also declare and initialize a variable in one line:
```go
var age int = 25
```

Type Inference

Go supports type inference, where the compiler determines the type based on the value assigned. This means you can simply declare a variable and assign it a value without specifying its type:

```go
age := 25
```

The `:=` operator is a shorthand that initializes a variable and infers its type, making variable declarations concise and readable.

Scope of Variables

The scope of a variable determines where it can be accessed within your code. In Go, variables can have global or local scopes. A variable declared outside of any function is a global variable, whereas one declared within a function is local to that function. It's essential to understand scope to avoid conflicts and maintain clear code.

1.2 Understanding Constants### What is a Constant?
A constant is similar to a variable, but unlike a variable, the value of a constant cannot change during the execution of a program. Constants provide clarity and reliability in code, representing fixed values that could be used throughout your program.

Declaring Constants in Go

In Go, you declare constants using the `const` keyword. Here's how you do it:

```go
const pi = 3.14
```

You can also specify the type of a constant:

```go
const pi float64 = 3.14
```

Grouping Constants

Go allows the grouping of constants, which can enhance organization and readability. You can group constants by enclosing them in parentheses:

```go
const (
weekday  = 7
weekend  = 2
totalDays = 365
)
```

This feature is particularly useful when defining related constants, making code easier to read and manage. ## 1.3 Data Types
The data type of a variable or constant defines the kind of data it can hold. Go is a statically typed language, which means you must declare the type of variables before they can be used. Here are the primary data types in Go:

Basic Types: `int`, `float64`, `string`, `bool`
Composite Types: `array`, `struct`, `slice`, `map`, `channel`
Function Types: Types that define functions

Choosing the correct data type for your variable or constant is crucial for performance and accuracy. For example, using an `int` for counting items is appropriate, whereas using a `float64` would be suitable for precision calculations like currency.

1.4 Best Practices

When working with variables and constants in Go, there

are several best practices to keep in mind:

Use Descriptive Names: Choose meaningful names for your variables and constants. This will make your code more readable and maintainable.

Limit Scope: Keep variables as local as possible. This helps prevent unintended side effects and makes your code easier to debug.

Immutable Values: Use constants for values that do not change. This promotes safer code and can prevent accidental modifications.

Group Related Constants: When you have multiple related constants, group them together. This enhances code organization and comprehension.

Consistency: Follow Go's conventions for naming. For example, Go typically uses camelCase for variable names and CapitalizedCase for exported constants.

Understanding variables and constants is foundational for mastering Go. They are not just essential for writing functional code; they are pivotal in developing efficient, readable, and maintainable applications. As you explore additional concepts in Go, keep in mind the significance of these building blocks and apply best practices to enhance your coding journey.

In the upcoming chapters, we will dive into control structures, functions, and more advanced features of Go. Each concept will build upon our understanding of these essential elements, guiding you to become proficient in Go programming.

Chapter 3: Exploring Go Data Types

This chapter delves into the various data types available in Go, categorizing them into primitive types, composite types, and reference types. We will also cover the concept of type conversion and how it impactsour programs.

3.1 Primitive Data Types

Primitive data types are the building blocks of data manipulation in Go. They represent single pieces of data and provide the simplest ways to handle information. Go has several primary primitive data types, each serving a specific purpose:

3.1.1 Boolean

The `bool` type is used to represent a binary state: true or false. It is commonly used for control flow statements, such as `if` and `for`.

```go
var isActive bool = trueif isActive {
fmt.Println("User is active.")
}
```

3.1.2 Numeric Types

Go has a rich set of numeric types that can be categorized into integers and floating-point numbers:

Integers:

`int`: The size of this type is platform-dependent (either 32 or 64 bits).

`int8`, `int16`, `int32`, `int64`: Signed integer types of varying sizes.

`uint`, `uint8`, `uint16`, `uint32`, `uint64`: Unsigned integer types corresponding to their signedequivalents.

```go
var x int = 10
var y float64 = 20.5
```

Floating-point:

`float32`: 32-bit floating-point number.

`float64`: 64-bit floating-point number (the default type for floating-point literals).### 3.1.3 Complex Types

Go also includes complex number types that can hold both real and imaginary parts:

`complex64`: A complex number with float32 real and imaginary parts.

`complex128`: A complex number with float64 real and imaginary parts.

```go
c := complex(1.0, 2.0) // Represents 1 + 2i realPart :=
real(c)
imaginaryPart := imag(c)
```

3.1.4 Strings

The `string` type represents a sequence of UTF-8 encoded characters. Strings in Go are immutable, meaningonce created, their contents cannot be changed.

```go
var greeting string = "Hello, World!"fmt.Println(greeting)
```

3.2 Composite Data Types

Composite data types allow the grouping of multiple values into a single entity. Go provides several powerful composite types:

3.2.1 Arrays

An array is a fixed-size sequence of elements of the same type. The size of the array must be specified at thetime of declaration.

```go
var numbers [5]int = [5]int{1, 2, 3, 4, 5}
```

3.2.2 Slices

Unlike arrays, slices are dynamically-sized and more flexible. A slice is a descriptor for a segment of anarray.

```go
var fruits []string = []string{"apple", "banana", "cherry"}
fruits = append(fruits, "date") // slices can grow in size
```

3.2.3 Maps

Maps are Go's built-in associative data type, allowing the storage of key-value pairs. They are unorderedcollections.

```go
ages := map[string]int{"Alice": 30,
"Bob":   25,
}
fmt.Println(ages["Alice"])
```

3.2.4 Structs

Structs are composite types that group together variables of different types under a single name. They are especially useful for defining complex data structures representing real-world entities.

```go
type Person struct {Name string
Age int
}
john := Person{Name: "John", Age: 30}
```

3.3 Reference Data Types

Reference types in Go store references to the underlying data rather than the data itself. This includes slices, maps, channels, and function types. Understanding references is vital for effective memory management and performance optimization.

3.3.1 Pointers

Pointers hold the memory address of a variable. They provide a way to reference data directly and are essential for certain programming techniques, such as modifying function arguments.

```go
var x int = 58 var ptr *int = &x
fmt.Println(*ptr) // Dereferences ptr to access the value at the address it points to.
```

47

3.4 Type Conversion

Go is a statically typed language, which means the data type of a variable is known at compile time. Type conversion is the explicit conversion from one type to another. This is crucial for ensuring that data types are compatible during operations.

```go
var i int = 10
var f float64 = float64(i) // Convert int to float64
```

Understanding the various data types in Go is foundational to effective programming in this language. From simple Boolean and numeric types to more complex structures like slices, maps, and structs, Go provides a rich type system that enables you to model your data accurately and efficiently. Through the proper use of these data types, you can write clearer, more maintainable, and more efficient code. As we proceed through the rest of this book, we will build upon these concepts and explore how to leverage Go's data types in practical applications.

Primitive Types: Numbers, Strings, and Booleans in Go

Go, also known as Golang, is a statically typed, compiled programming language designed for simplicity, efficiency, and productivity. At the core of Go's type system are its primitive types, which serve as the building blocks for creating data structures and implementing algorithms. This chapter focuses on three fundamental primitive types: numbers, strings, and booleans. Understanding these types is essential for every Go programmer as they form the basis for data manipulation and control flow in Go applications.

1. Numbers

Go provides several numeric data types, divided into three main categories: integer types, floating-point types, and complex types.

1.1 Integer Types

Go has several signed and unsigned integer types that can represent whole numbers. The signed typesinclude:

`int8`: 8-bit signed integer
`int16`: 16-bit signed integer
`int32`: 32-bit signed integer
`int64`: 64-bit signed integer
`int`: platform-dependent signed integer (either 32 or 64 bits)Unsigned types are:
`uint8`: 8-bit unsigned integer
`uint16`: 16-bit unsigned integer
`uint32`: 32-bit unsigned integer
`uint64`: 64-bit unsigned integer
`uint`: platform-dependent unsigned integer Integer values can be declared and used as follows:
```go
var a int = 42 var b uint = 27
var c int64 = 10000000000
```

Go also supports various operations with integers, such as addition, subtraction, multiplication, and division. Be aware of the potential for overflow or underflow when operating on smaller integer types (e.g., `int8`), as they can only hold a limited range of values.

1.2 Floating-point Types

For representing numbers with fractional parts, Go provides floating-point types:

`float32`: 32-bit IEEE-754 floating-point
`float64`: 64-bit IEEE-754 floating-point

When declaring floating-point variables, you can use the `float64` type for greater precision:

```go
var price float64 = 19.99 var distance float32 = 3.5
```

Go supports standard arithmetic operations and additional functions from the `math` package for more complex calculations, such as trigonometric functions or logarithms.

1.3 Complex Numbers

Go also supports complex numbers using the `complex64` and `complex128` types. A complex number consists of a real part and an imaginary part:

```go
```

```go
var c1 complex64 = 1 + 2i
var c2 complex128 = 3.0 + 4.0i
```

You can perform arithmetic operations on complex numbers similarly to integers and floating-pointnumbers.

2. Strings

Strings in Go are a sequence of bytes, representing UTF-8 encoded text. Unlike some languages, strings in Go are immutable, meaning they cannot be changed after they are created. This characteristic can lead to more predictable behavior and performance optimizations.

2.1 String Creation and Manipulation

You can declare strings using double quotes (`"`):

```go
var greeting string = "Hello, World!"
```

Strings can also be defined using backticks (` ` `) to create raw string literals, which preserve whitespace and escape sequences:

```go
var rawGreeting string = `Hello,World!`
```

You can concatenate strings using the `+` operator:

```go
var name string = "Alice"
var message string = greeting + " " + name
```

2.2 String Methods

Go provides a rich set of built-in functions for string manipulation, found in the `strings` package. Some commonly used functions include:

`strings.Contains(s, substr)`: checks if `s` contains `substr`
`strings.ToUpper(s)`: converts `s` to uppercase
`strings.Split(s, delim)`: splits `s` into substrings based on the delimiter `delim`Example usage:
```go
import "strings"

greeting := "Hello, Golang!"
if strings.Contains(greeting, "Golang") {
fmt.Println("Welcome to the Go programming language!")
}
```

3. Booleans

The boolean type in Go has two possible values: `true` and `false`. Booleans are primarily used for control flow, conditions, and loops.

3.1 Boolean Variables

You can declare boolean variables as follows:

```go
var isActive bool = true var isAdmin bool = false
```

3.2 Boolean Expressions

Booleans often result from comparisons and logical operations. The typical comparison operators (`==`, `!=`, `<`, `>`, `<=`, `>=`) yield boolean results:

```go
a := 5
b := 10
isGreater := (a > b) // falseisEqual := (a == b)  // false
```

Logical operators `&&` (AND), `||` (OR), and `!` (NOT) can be used to combine boolean values:

```go
isTrue := true isFalse := false
result := isTrue && !isFalse // true
```

Primitive types in Go—numbers, strings, and booleans—are fundamental to mastering the language. They form the basis for data storage and manipulation, enabling developers to build robust and efficient applications. By understanding these types and their characteristics, you will be well-equipped to leverage Go's strengths in developing high-performance software. As you progress in your Go programming journey, keep exploring the rich ecosystem of libraries and tools that complement these primitive types, enhancing your coding experience.

Working with Composite Types: Arrays, Slices, and Maps in Go

This chapter delves into three fundamental composite types in Go: arrays, slices, and maps. Understandingthese types is crucial for effective programming in Go as they provide the foundation for storing and manipulating collections of data.

1. Arrays

Definition and Syntax

An array in Go is a fixed-size, ordered collection of elements of the same type. The syntax for declaring an array is as follows:

```go
var arrayName [size]elementType
```

For example, to declare an array of five integers, you would write:

```go
var numbers [5]int
```

```
```

Initialization

Arrays can be initialized at the time of declaration. You can initialize an array by specifying its elements within curly braces:

```go
var numbers = [5]int{1, 2, 3, 4, 5}
```

Additionally, Go allows for shorthand declarations with implicit sizing through the use of `...`, whichautomatically determines the length:

```go
numbers := [...]int{1, 2, 3, 4, 5}
```

Accessing and Modifying Arrays

Elements in an array can be accessed using their index, which starts at 0. You can change an element byassigning a new value to a specific index:

```go
numbers[0] = 10 // Change the first element to 10
fmt.Println(numbers) // Output: [10 2 3 4 5]
```

Limitations of Arrays

While arrays are straightforward to use, they come with limitations. The most significant one is their fixed size. Once created, the size of an array cannot be changed, which can lead to inefficiency in certain situations. For more flexible data structures, slices are typically preferred.

2. Slices

Definition and Syntax

A slice is a dynamically-sized, flexible view into the elements of an array. It is much more versatile than an array and can be resized. The syntax for declaring a slice is as follows:

```go
var sliceName []elementType
```

For example, to declare a slice of integers:

```go
var numbers []int
```

Creating Slices

You can create slices using the `make` function or by slicing existing arrays. The `make` function allows you to specify the length and capacity:

```go
```

```go
slice := make([]int, 5) // Creates a slice of length 5 with zero values
```

To create a slice from an existing array, you can use the `array[start:end]` syntax, which gives you a subset of the original array:

```go
array := [5]int{1, 2, 3, 4, 5}
slice := array[1:4] // slice now contains [2, 3, 4]
```

Appending to Slices

One of the key features of slices is their ability to grow dynamically. You can append elements to a slice using the built-in `append` function:

```go
slice = append(slice, 6) // Appends 6 to the slice
```

Copying Slices

If you need to copy a slice, you can do so with the `copy` function. This will create a new slice and copy the elements from the original slice:

```go
original := []int{1, 2, 3}
copySlice := make([]int, len(original))
copy(copySlice, original) // copySlice now holds a
```

separate copy of original
```

## 3. Maps

### Definition and Syntax

A map is an unordered collection of key-value pairs, where each key is unique. It provides an efficient wayto store and retrieve data. The syntax for declaring a map is:

```go
var mapName map[keyType]valueType
```

For example, to declare a map where the key is a string and the value is an integer:

```go
var ages map[string]int
```

Initialization

Maps must be initialized using the `make` function:

```go
ages = make(map[string]int)
```

You can also initialize a map with values at the time of declaration:
```

```go
ages := map[string]int{"Alice": 30, "Bob": 25}
```

Adding and Retrieving Elements

Adding key-value pairs to a map is straightforward. You simply assign a value to a key:

```go
ages["Charlie"] = 35
```

To retrieve a value, you access the map using the key:

```go
age := ages["Alice"] // age will be 30
```

Checking for Existence

When retrieving a value from a map, you can also check if the key exists:

```go
age, exists := ages["Eve"]if exists {
fmt.Println(age)
} else {
fmt.Println("Eve not found")
}
```

Deleting Elements

You can remove a key-value pair from a map using the `delete` function:

```go
delete(ages, "Bob") // Removes Bob from the map
```

Understanding composite types—arrays, slices, and maps—is essential in Go programming. Each type has its specific use cases, strengths, and limitations. Arrays are useful for fixed-size collections, slices offer flexibility and dynamic sizing, and maps provide an efficient way to associate keys with values.

As you work with these types, keep in mind the performance implications of each composite type as well as their memory management characteristics. Embracing these tools will significantly enhance your ability to manage data structures and write effective Go programs.

Chapter 4: Managing Program Flow in Go

Go, as a statically typed, compiled language designed for simplicity and efficiency, provides various constructs and idioms to control the flow of execution. This chapter will delve into the fundamental elements that govern program flow in Go, including conditionals, loops, and error handling. By mastering these constructs, you can write more robust and expressive programs.

4.1 Control Flow Statements ### 4.1.1 Conditional Statements

Conditional statements allow you to execute different blocks of code based on certain conditions. In Go, the primary conditional statement is the `if` statement, which can be used to execute code only when a specified condition is true.

```go
package mainimport "fmt"
func main() { number := 10 if number > 0 {
fmt.Println("The number is positive.")
} else if number < 0 {
fmt.Println("The number is negative.")
} else {
fmt.Println("The number is zero.")
}
}
```

In this example, the program checks whether the variable

`number` is greater than, less than, or equal to zero, providing appropriate feedback for each scenario. Go also supports a unique feature called the "if statement with a short declaration" which allows you to declare and initialize a variable in the conditionitself:

```go
if err := doSomething(); err != nil { fmt.Println("Error:", err)
}
```

4.1.2 Switch Statements

For scenarios requiring multiple branches based on the same variable or expression, a `switch` statement isoften more elegant and efficient than multiple `if` statements. The `switch` statement automatically breaks after each case, eliminating the need for additional `break` statements common in other languages.

```go
func dayType(day string) {

switch day {
case "Saturday", "Sunday": fmt.Println("It's the weekend!")
default:
fmt.Println("It's a weekday.")
}
}
```

This function categorizes the day as either a weekday or a weekend, demonstrating how `switch` statements can simplify decision-making.

4.2 Looping Constructs

Go offers several ways to repeat a block of code, with the `for` loop being the only looping construct available. The `for` loop can be used in various forms: traditional iteration with a counter, range-based iteration, and as a while loop.

4.2.1 Traditional For Loop

The traditional `for` loop structure in Go consists of three components: initialization, condition, and poststatement.

```go
for i := 0; i < 5; i++ {fmt.Println(i)
}
```

In this loop, `i` starts from 0 and increments until it reaches 5, printing each value to the console. ### 4.2.2 Range-Based For Loop
The `range` keyword allows iterating over various data structures such as arrays, slices, maps, and channels.

```go
fruits := []string{"apple", "banana", "cherry"} for index, value := range fruits {
fmt.Printf("Index: %d, Value: %s\n", index, value)
}
```

```
```

This loop iterates over the `fruits` slice, providing both the index and value of each element. ### 4.2.3 Infinite Loops
Sometimes, you may want to create a loop that executes indefinitely, which can be accomplished with `for {}`. You must ensure to implement a mechanism to break out of the loop.

```go
counter := 0for {
fmt.Println("Counter:", counter)counter++

if counter > 5 {break
}
}
```

In this example, the loop continues until `counter` exceeds 5, demonstrating how to safely manage infinite loops.

4.3 Error Handling

Error handling is integral to managing program flow, especially in a language like Go that emphasizes simplicity. In Go, error handling is typically achieved through the use of multiple return values, with the last return value being of type `error`.

```go
func divide(a, b int) (int, error) {if b == 0 {
return 0, fmt.Errorf("division by zero")
```

```
}
return a / b, nil
}

func main() {
result, err := divide(10, 0)if err != nil {
fmt.Println("Error:", err)return
}
fmt.Println("Result:", result)
}
```

In the `divide` function, we check for division by zero and return an error if this occurs. In the `main` function, we handle this error gracefully, providing feedback to the user.

Effective management of program flow is essential in Go programming, enabling developers to control how the program responds to data and user input. Understanding and utilizing conditional statements, loops, and error handling constructs will enhance your ability to write clear, efficient, and maintainable code. As you continue to develop your Go programming skills, always strive to write code that is not only functional but also easy to read and understand. In the next chapter, we will explore functions in Go, further enhancing your ability to structure and organize your code.

Conditional Statements and Loops in Go

Go, also known as Golang, is a statically typed, compiled language designed for simplicity and efficiency. One of the core aspects of any programming language is its ability to control the flow of execution through conditional statements and loops. In this chapter, we will explore these essential constructs in Go, providing clarity on their syntax and practical applications.

Conditional Statements

Conditional statements allow programmers to execute code based on certain conditions. In Go, the primary conditional statement is the `if` statement, followed by `else if` and `else` constructs. The syntax is straightforward and reminiscent of many other programming languages, yet it incorporates some unique aspects.

The `if` Statement

The basic structure of an `if` statement in Go looks like this:

```go
if condition {
// Code to execute if the condition is true
}
```

Here's a simple example:

```go
package mainimport "fmt"
func main() {age := 18
if age >= 18 {
fmt.Println("You are eligible to vote.")
}
}
```

In this example, the program checks if `age` is greater than or equal to 18, and if true, it prints a message to the console.

The `else if` and `else` Statements

To handle multiple conditions, Go allows the use of `else if` followed by an optional `else` block:

```go
if condition1 {
// Code if condition1 is true
} else if condition2 {
// Code if condition2 is true

} else {
// Code if none of the above conditions are true
}
```

Here's an example:

```go
package mainimport "fmt"
```

```go
func main() {score := 85

if score >= 90 { fmt.Println("Grade: A")
} else if score >= 75 { fmt.Println("Grade: B")
} else if score >= 60 { fmt.Println("Grade: C")
} else {
fmt.Println("Grade: D")
}
}
```

In this case, the program evaluates the `score` variable and prints the corresponding grade based on the score range.

The `switch` Statement

Another way to handle multiple conditions is to use a `switch` statement, which can be more elegant and easier to read. The syntax is as follows:

```go
switch variable {case value1:
// Code if variable == value1case value2:
// Code if variable == value2default:
// Code if none of the above cases match
}
```

Here's an example:

```go
package mainimport "fmt"
```

```go
func main() {
day := "Tuesday"

switch day { case "Monday":
fmt.Println("Start of the week!")case "Friday":
fmt.Println("Almost the weekend!") case "Saturday",
"Sunday":
fmt.Println("Weekend!")default:
fmt.Println("Midweek day.")
}
}
```

This program uses a `switch` statement to print different messages based on the value of `day`.## Loops
Loops are critical for executing repetitive tasks. Go offers several looping constructs, the most common being the `for` loop, which is versatile and can be used in multiple ways.

The `for` Loop

The `for` loop is Go's only looping construct. Its basic format looks like this:

```go
for initialization; condition; post {
// Code to execute on each iteration
}
```

Here's a straightforward example:

```go
package main
import "fmt" func main() {
for i := 0; i < 5; i++ { fmt.Println("Iteration:", i)
}
}
```

In this program, the loop iterates from 0 to 4, printing the current iteration number.#### Infinite Loops
If the condition of a `for` loop is always true, you create an infinite loop:

```go
for {
// Code to execute indefinitely
}
```

This can be useful in certain circumstances, such as waiting for input or continually processing data until a specific condition breaks the loop.

Looping Over Collections

Go provides a convenient way to iterate over slices and maps using the `for` range construct:

```go
slice := []int{1, 2, 3, 4, 5}
for index, value := range slice { fmt.Println("Index:", index, "Value:", value)
}
```

```
` ` `
```

This iterates over `slice`, printing both the index and the value for each element.### Break and Continue
Within loops, you can control the flow using `break` and `continue` statements. The `break` statement exits the loop entirely, while `continue` skips the current iteration and moves to the next one:

```go
for i := 0; i < 10; i++ {if i%2 == 0 {
continue // Skip even numbers
}
fmt.Println(i) // Print odd numbers only
}
```

In this chapter, we explored the fundamental concepts of conditional statements and loops in the Go programming language. Understanding these constructs is crucial for controlling the flow of your applications and executing logic based on different conditions. As you practice coding in Go, try to implement these statements in various problems, solidifying your knowledge and preparing yourself for more advanced programming techniques. The power of Go lies in its simplicity and efficiency, enabling youto write clean, readable, and effective code.

Error Handling: Best Practices for Robust Code in Go

Error handling is a critical aspect of software

development, and it becomes even more pronounced in the Go programming language. Go adopts a unique approach to error handling that emphasizes simplicity, clarity, and explicitness. In this chapter, we will explore best practices for effectively handling errors in your Go applications, helping you write more robust, maintainable, and user-friendly code.

Understanding Go's Error Type

In Go, errors are represented using the built-in `error` interface, which is defined as follows:

```go
type error interface {Error() string
}
```

An error in Go is any type that implements this interface. Most commonly, errors are created using the `errors.New` function or the `fmt.Errorf` function. This approach promotes a clear distinction between error handling and the normal flow of the program.

Sample Error Creation

Here's how you might create a simple error in Go:

```go
package main

import ( "errors""fmt"
)
```

```go
func doSomething() error {
return errors.New("an error occurred")
}

func main() {
if err := doSomething(); err != nil {fmt.Println("Error:",
err)
}
}
```

Best Practices for Error Handling ### 1. Return Errors Explicitly

In Go, it is conventional to return an error as the last return value of a function. This clearly signals to thecaller that they should expect and handle an error.

```go
func readFile(filename string) ([]byte, error) {data, err :=
ioutil.ReadFile(filename)
if err != nil {
return nil, fmt.Errorf("unable to read file %s: %w",
filename, err)
}
return data, nil
}
```

2. Use `fmt.Errorf` with `%w` for Wrapping Errors

When handling errors, it's essential to provide context.

73

Using `fmt.Errorf` with the `%w` verb allows you to wrap errors, preserving the original error while adding helpful context.

```go
if err := someOperation(); err != nil {
return fmt.Errorf("failed to perform some operation: %w", err)
}
```

3. Handle Errors Early

Always handle errors as soon as possible after they occur. This prevents the propagation of errors through your application and facilitates easier debugging.

```go
file, err := os.Open("nonexistent.txt")if err != nil {
log.Fatalf("failed to open file: %v", err)
}
// Subsequent operations on the file
```

4. Differentiate Between Expected and Unexpected Errors

Not all errors are created equal. It's important to differentiate between expected errors (e.g., a user entering invalid input) and unexpected errors (e.g., a system failure). Consider using sentinel errors or error types to distinguish these cases.

```go
var ErrNotFound = errors.New("not found")

func findItem(id int) (Item, error) {
if item, found := database[id]; found {return item, nil
}
return Item{}, ErrNotFound
}
```

5. Create Custom Error Types

For more complex applications, creating custom error types can provide additional context about errors. Custom error types can embed additional information, such as error codes.

```go
type MyError struct {Code int
Message string
}

func (e *MyError) Error() string {
return fmt.Sprintf("Code: %d, Message: %s", e.Code, e.Message)
}

func doRiskyThing() error {
return &MyError{Code: 404, Message: "not found"}
}
```

6. Log Errors Appropriately

75

Logging errors is essential for diagnosing issues in production systems. Use logging libraries that suit your needs, and ensure that logs contain enough context to facilitate troubleshooting.

```go
if err != nil {
log.Printf("Error encountered: %v", err)
}
```

7. Avoid Panic for Normal Errors

Go has built-in support for panics, but it should be reserved for unrecoverable errors. Use panics sparingly and never for normal error handling.

8. Document Error Behavior

Well-documented functions make it easier for other developers (and your future self) to understand what to expect regarding error handling. Clearly state under which conditions your function might return an error.

```go
// AddItem adds a new item to the collection.
// It returns an error if the item already exists. func AddItem(item Item) error {
// Function implementation
}
```

Effective error handling is a hallmark of robust software. Go's straightforward error handling pattern encourages developers to write clear, manageable, and maintainable code. By following the best practices outlined in this chapter—returning and wrapping errors, differentiating between types of errors, logging appropriately, and documenting your code—you can create Go applications that are resilient, informative, and easy to debug. Remember that error handling is not just about managing failures; it's a fundamental part of building quality software.

Chapter 5: Writing Modular Code with Functionsin Go

In Go, one of the core principles that helps developers achieve modularity is the use of functions. Functions not only allow us to break down our code into manageable parts, but they also provide reusable building blocks that can improve both the readability and maintainability of our applications. In this chapter, we will explore how to effectively leverage functions in Go to write modular code.

5.1 Understanding Functions

At its core, a function in Go is a block of code designed to perform a specific task. You can think of a function as a mini-program that you can call from different parts of your application to perform a certain action or compute a value.

Function Declaration

A function in Go is defined using the `func` keyword, followed by a name, parentheses for parameters, a return type, and a body that contains the code to be executed. Here is the basic syntax:

```go
func functionName(parameter1 type, parameter2 type)
returnType {
// Function bodyreturn value
}
```

Let's consider an example:

```go
func add(a int, b int) int {return a + b
}
```

In this example, we defined a function called `add` that takes two integer parameters and returns their sum. ### Calling Functions
Once a function is declared, you can call it from anywhere in your program. Here's how you would use the `add` function:

```go
result := add(3, 5) fmt.Println(result) // Output: 8
```

5.2 Function Parameters and Return Types

One of the strengths of functions is their ability to accept parameters and return values. This allows functions to operate on different data inputs and produce output accordingly.

Multiple Parameters

Go supports multiple parameters of varying types. These can be defined in a single line or spread across multiple lines for clarity:

```go
func multiply(x int, y float64) float64 {return float64(x) * y
}
```

When calling this function, you need to make sure the argument types match the parameters:

```go
result := multiply(6, 3.5) fmt.Println(result) // Output: 21.0
```

Named Return Values

Go allows you to define named return values, which can enhance code clarity. This can be particularly useful in functions with multiple return values.

```go
func divide(num1, num2 float64) (result float64, err error) {if num2 == 0 {
err = fmt.Errorf("division by zero")return
}
result = num1 / num2return
}
```

```
```

In this example, the function `divide` returns both a result and an error. If an error occurs, the function will populate the `err` variable without needing an explicit `return` statement.

5.3 Variadic Functions

Another powerful feature in Go is the ability to define variadic functions: functions that can accept a variable number of arguments. This is especially useful when the number of inputs isn't known at compile-time.

To declare a variadic function, use an ellipsis (`...`) before the type in the function's parameter list:

```go
func sum(numbers ...int) int {total := 0
for _, num := range numbers {total += num
}
return total
}
```

You can call this function with any number of arguments:

```go
total := sum(1, 2, 3, 4, 5) fmt.Println(total) // Output: 15
```

5.4 Higher-Order Functions

Go's first-class functions allow you to pass functions as arguments to other functions, return them from functions, and assign them to variables. These are often referred to as higher-order functions and can lead toelegant solutions in programming.

Here's an example of a higher-order function that takes another function as a parameter:

```go
func applyOperation(a, b int, operation func(int, int) int) int {return operation(a, b)
}
```

You could then pass the `add` function as an argument:

```go
result := applyOperation(4, 5, add) fmt.Println(result) // Output: 9
```

5.5 Best Practices for Writing Functions

Creating effective functions goes beyond just writing code. There are several best practices worthconsidering:

Single Responsibility: A function should perform one task or action. This makes the function easier to understand, test, and reuse.

Meaningful Names: Choose descriptive names for your functions and parameters. A function shouldconvey what it does just by its name.

Keep it Small: Functions should be small enough that they can be understood at a glance. If a function grows large, consider breaking it into smaller functions.

Error Handling: Handle errors gracefully within your functions. Returning error values instead of panicking allows the calling code to respond appropriately.

Commenting: While code should be self-explanatory, comments can clarify complex logic. Use comments judiciously to enhance understanding rather than clutter.

In this chapter, we explored the foundational aspects of writing modular code using functions in Go. Functions help in structuring your codebase and provide a means for code reuse. By mastering how to define, use, and effectively manage functions, you can build applications that are not only efficient but also easier to maintain and extend.

As you continue to develop your skills in Go, keep practicing these principles of modularity, and leverage the power of functions to create clean, robust, and scalable applications. In the next chapter, we will delve

into more advanced concepts, including interfaces and their role in promoting modular design patterns in Go.

Function Declarations and Return Values in Go

In Go (often referred to as Golang), functions are a cornerstone of the language, enabling code reuse and providing a clear structure. This chapter explores how to declare functions, their syntax, and how to handle return values effectively.

Understanding Function Declarations

A function in Go is defined using the `func` keyword followed by the function name, parameters, and return types. The basic syntax for a function declaration is as follows:

```go
func functionName(parameter1 type1, parameter2 type2) returnType {
// function body
}
```

Basic Syntax

Let's take a closer look at the components of a function declaration:

Keyword: The declaration starts with `func`, signaling the start of a function.
Function Name: This is the identifier for the function. It should be descriptive of the function's purpose.
Parameters: Inside parentheses, you can define

parameters that the function accepts, along with their types (e.g., `x int, y int`).
Return Type: After parameters, you specify the return type(s). This can be a single type or multipletypes.
Function Body: Enclosed in curly braces `{}`, this contains the code that executes when the functionis called.

Example of a Simple Function

Here's a simple function that adds two integers:

```go
func add(x int, y int) int {return x + y
}
```

In this example:
The function `add` takes two parameters, both of type `int`.
It returns an `int`, which is the sum of the two numbers.
Multiple Return Values
One of the unique features of Go is the ability to return multiple values from a function. This is particularlyuseful for functions that need to return both a result and an error.

Example with Multiple Return Values

Here is an example illustrating multiple return values:

```go
func divide(x, y float64) (float64, error) {if y == 0 {
return 0, fmt.Errorf("division by zero")
```

```go
}
    return x / y, nil
}
```

In this example:
The `divide` function returns a `float64` result and an `error`.
If the divisor `y` is zero, the function returns an error; otherwise, it returns the quotient and `nil` for theerror.

Handling Return Values

When calling a function that returns multiple values, you can use the following syntax:

```go
result, err := divide(10, 2)if err != nil {
fmt.Println("Error:", err)
} else {
fmt.Println("Result:", result)
}
```

In the snippet above:
The returned values from `divide` are assigned to `result` and `err`.
Error checking is implemented to handle any potential issues before using the result.## Named Return Values
Go also allows the use of named return values. This feature can make your code more readable and easier to understand. You can declare return types in the function signature, and they will be treated as variables.

Example with Named Return Values

```go
func calculate(x, y float64) (sum float64, product float64) {sum = x + y
product = x * y
return // with named return values, you can omit the names
}
```

In this case:
The function `calculate` has named return values `sum` and `product`.
The `return` statement at the end uses the named return values, making it clear what is being returned. ## Recursion and Functions Functions in Go can also call themselves, leading to a programming concept known as recursion. While recursion can be powerful for certain problems, it's essential to ensure there's a base case to prevent infiniteloops.

Example of a Recursive Function

Here's a simple example of a recursive function that computes the factorial of a number:

```go
func factorial(n int) int {if n == 0 {
return 1
}
return n * factorial(n-1)
```

```
}
```
Understanding the Base Case In the `factorial` function:

The base case is `if n == 0`, which prevents the function from calling itself indefinitely.

For positive integers, it multiplies `n` by the factorial of `n - 1`, building up the result until the base case is reached.

Function declarations and return values are fundamental concepts in Go programming. Mastering these will enable you to write clear, efficient, and reusable code. As you become proficient with functions, you'll find that they are not only integral to structuring your application but also essential in maintaining clean and understandable code. In the next chapter, we will explore more advanced topics such as closures, higher- order functions, and the implications of concurrency in function design.

Advanced Function Techniques: Closures and Recursion

Go, being a modern programming language, brings

unique features to the table, particularly in its first-class function capabilities, closures, and recursion techniques. This chapter aims to dive into these advanced function techniques, specifically focusing on closures and recursion in Go, empowering you with the tools needed for more complex programming scenarios.

Understanding Closures

A closure is a function that captures the environment in which it was declared. This means that the functionretains access to the variables and parameters of its surrounding scope, even after that scope has finished executing. Closures are particularly useful for creating function factories or for managing state in an otherwise stateless way.

Creating Closures in Go

Let's take a look at how closures are implemented in Go through an example. Consider the following codesnippet:

```go
package mainimport "fmt"
func main() {
counter := createCounter() fmt.Println(counter()) // Outputs: 1 fmt.Println(counter()) // Outputs: 2 fmt.Println(counter()) // Outputs: 3
}

func createCounter() func() int {
count := 0 // This variable is captured by the closure
return func() int {
```

```
count++ // Incrementing the captured variable return
count
}
}
```

In this example, the `createCounter` function returns another function that increments and returns an internal counter. The `count` variable is preserved across calls to the returned function, showcasing the closure's ability to capture and maintain state.

Applications of Closures

Closures are widely used in various programming patterns such as:

Function Factories: As shown in the previous example, closures allow you to create specialized functions on the fly.
Callbacks: Often used in asynchronous programming, closures can encapsulate callback functions that hold context about their execution state.
Data Encapsulation: Closures can help encapsulate data and expose only the necessary functions, promoting better data hiding and modularity.

Understanding and effectively using closures will enable you to write more modular, cleaner, and reusable code in Go.

Delving into Recursion

Recursion is a powerful programming technique where a function calls itself to solve smaller subproblems of a larger problem. This can simplify code and make it easier to understand when used correctly.

Implementing Recursion in Go

To illustrate recursion, let's examine a classic example: calculating the factorial of a number.

```go
package mainimport "fmt"
func main() {n := 5
result := factorial(n)
fmt.Printf("Factorial of %d is %d\n", n, result)
}

func factorial(n int) int {if n == 0 { // Base case
return 1
}
return n * factorial(n-1) // Recursive call
}
```

In this example, the `factorial` function computes the factorial of `n` by calling itself with a decremented value until it reaches the base case, where `n` equals zero. Each recursive call builds up the solution until the function unwinds, calculating the result.

Pros and Cons of Recursion

While recursion can lead to elegant solutions, it has its

trade-offs:

- **Pros**:
Clarity: Recursive solutions often mirror the mathematical definitions of problems, making them easy to understand.
Reduced Boilerplate: Recursion eliminates the need for explicit loops in some situations, leading to cleaner code.

- **Cons**:
Performance: Recursive calls can lead to a larger stack depth and may result in stack overflow for deep recursion.
Overhead: Each function call incurs overhead, and recursive functions can be less efficient than iterative solutions for certain problems.

Tail Call Optimization

Go does not support tail call optimization, which means that deep recursion could result in stack overflow.As such, it is crucial to be cautious when implementing recursive algorithms in production code. Iterative solutions can often be more efficient and safe, especially for problems that might involve deep recursion.

Combining Closures and Recursion

Combining closures and recursion can yield particularly powerful patterns. One practical example is implementing memoization, a technique where you store the results of expensive function calls and returnthe cached result when the same inputs occur again. This can significantly optimize recursive algorithms.

Here's an example of a memoized Fibonacci function:

```go
package mainimport "fmt"
func main() {
fib   :=   memoizedFibonacci()   fmt.Println(fib(10))   //
Outputs: 55
}

func   memoizedFibonacci()   func(int)   int   {   cache   :=
make(map[int]int)

return func(n int) int {if n <= 1 {
return n
}
if val, found := cache[n]; found {return val
}
cache[n]       =       memoizedFibonacci()(n-1)       +
memoizedFibonacci()(n-2)return cache[n]
}
}
```

In this example, we encapsulate the Fibonacci logic in a closure while providing memoization capabilities. The cached results improve the efficiency of the recursive function calls, showcasing the power of combining closures with recursion.

Mastering closures and recursion in Go can elevate your programming capabilities, allowing you to tackle complex problems with elegance and efficiency. By understanding how to create and utilize closures effectively, tapping into the strengths of recursion, and combining both techniques for optimization, you position yourself to write robust and scalable applications. As you continue your journey in Go, embrace these advanced function techniques, and leverage them to enhance your coding prowess and problem-solvingskills.

Chapter 6: Leveraging Methods and Interfaces inGo

Go, often referred to as Golang, is a statically typed, compiled language designed by Google that emphasizes simplicity and efficiency. One of the powerful features of Go is its support for methods and interfaces, whichenable developers to write flexible and modular code. In this chapter, we will explore how to effectively leverage methods and interfaces in Go to create clean, maintainable, and reusable code.

6.1 Understanding Methods

In Go, methods are functions that are associated with a specific type. They allow you to define behaviors foryour types and are defined with a receiver argument that acts as a context for the method's operations.

6.1.1 Defining Methods

A method is defined using the following syntax:

```go
func            (receiverType            receiverName) methodName(parameters) returnType {
// method body
}
```

Here's an example of defining a method for a struct type:

```go
type Circle struct {Radius float64
}

// Method to calculate the area of the circlefunc (c Circle)
Area() float64 {
return math.Pi * c.Radius * c.Radius
}
```

In this example, `Area` is a method of the `Circle` type
and can be called on an instance of `Circle`. ### 6.1.2
Pointer vs. Value Receivers
Methods can have either value receivers or pointer
receivers. A value receiver receives a copy of the value,
whereas a pointer receiver receives a reference to the
value.

Using pointer receivers allows you to modify the receiver's
value inside the method:

```go
func (c *Circle) Scale(factor float64) {c.Radius *= factor
}
```

In this example, `Scale` modifies the `Radius` of `Circle`
without creating a copy.### 6.1.3 Method Sets
A key concept in Go is the method set, which is a
collection of methods defined for a type. This becomes
important when working with interfaces, as it lets Go
determine whether a type implements an interface based
on its method set.

6.2 Interfaces in Go

Interfaces are a core component of Go's type system and enable polymorphic behavior. An interface defines a contract that types must follow, specifying a set of method signatures.

6.2.1 Defining Interfaces

To define an interface, you use the `type` keyword in conjunction with the `interface` keyword:

```go
type Shape interface {Area() float64
}
```

Any type that implements the methods defined in an interface automatically satisfies that interface, making it easy to write flexible and reusable code.

6.2.2 Implementing Interfaces

You can implement an interface by simply defining the required methods. For instance, let's implement the `Shape` interface with our `Circle` and also add a `Rectangle`:

```go
type Rectangle struct { Width, Height float64
}
```

```go
func (r Rectangle) Area() float64 { return r.Width *
r.Height
}
```

Now both `Circle` and `Rectangle` implement `Shape`, allowing you to work with them interchangeably in functions that accept `Shape`:

```go
func PrintArea(s Shape) { fmt.Println("Area:", s.Area())
}
```

6.2.3 Empty Interfaces

An empty interface, defined as `interface{}`, can hold values of any type, making it a powerful tool for building functions that can handle various types without the need for type assertion.

```go
func PrintValue(v interface{}) {fmt.Println("Value:", v)
}
```

While powerful, the use of empty interfaces should be done judiciously to avoid losing type information and to ensure type safety.

6.3 Embedding and Composition

Go encourages composition over inheritance, facilitating

code reuse and composition of types. You can embed one struct into another, allowing the outer struct to inherit methods from the inner struct.

6.3.1 Struct Embedding

The following example demonstrates struct embedding:

```go
type ShapeInfo struct {Name string
}

type Circle struct {ShapeInfo Radius float64
}

func (c Circle) Info() string {
return fmt.Sprintf("Shape: %s, Radius: %f", c.Name, c.Radius)
}
```

Here, `Circle` embeds `ShapeInfo`, gaining access to the `Name` field and the `Info()` method.### 6.3.2 Interface Composition
Interfaces can also be composed by embedding other interfaces:

```go
type Drawable interface {Draw()
}

type Shape interface {Area() float64 Drawable
}
```

99

```
```

In this case, any type that implements `Shape` must also implement `Draw()`. ## 6.4 Best Practices for Methods and Interfaces **Use Interfaces Liberally**: Interfaces are deeply integrated into Go's concurrency features, making them invaluable for designing your applications.

Keep Interfaces Small: Follow the Interface Segregation Principle by creating small, purpose-specific interfaces.

Favor Composition: Use struct embedding and interface composition to build flexible systems.

Document Interfaces and Methods: Clear documentation helps maintain understanding and usabilityof your code.

In this chapter, we explored the importance of methods and interfaces in Go, learning how to utilize them for creating effective and structured applications. Methods allow structs to exhibit behavior, while interfaces provide a powerful mechanism for abstraction and polymorphism. By understanding and leveraging these features, you can write cleaner, more maintainable code in Go. As we continue our journey through the Go programming language, remember that mastering these concepts opens up a world of possibilities for scalable application design.

Understanding Methods and Pointer Receivers in Go

This chapter explores the nuances of defining methods on

types, how receiver types affect method behavior, and the implications of using pointers versus values.

What are Methods in Go?

In Go, a method is simply a function that has a defined receiver. The receiver can be thought of as the context in which the method operates, allowing it to access the associated data for the receiving type. This is different from traditional object-oriented languages where methods belong explicitly to a class.

Defining a Method

To define a method in Go, one must first declare a receiver variable in the function signature. The receiver can be either a value type or a pointer type. Here's a simple example:

```go
package main

import (
"fmt"
)

// Define a struct type type Rectangle struct {
width float64height float64
}

// Method with value receiver
func (r Rectangle) Area() float64 {return r.width * r.height
}
```

```go
// Method with pointer receiver
func (r *Rectangle) Scale(factor float64) {r.width *= factor
r.height *= factor
}

func main() {
// Create a Rectangle instance
rect := Rectangle{width: 10, height: 5}

// Call the Area method fmt.Println("Area:", rect.Area())

// Scale the rectanglerect.Scale(2)

fmt.Println("New Area after scaling:", rect.Area())
}
```

In the example above, `Area` is a method with a value receiver, which means it works with a copy of the `Rectangle` instance. The `Scale` method, on the other hand, takes a pointer receiver, allowing it to modify the original `Rectangle`.

Value Receivers vs. Pointer Receivers

Understanding the difference between value receivers and pointer receivers can help you choose the appropriate method type based on the functionality you need.

Value Receivers

When a method is defined with a value receiver, Go

creates a copy of the receiver value when the method is invoked. This means that any modifications made to the receiver within the method do not affect the originalvalue. This can be useful for methods that are meant only to read data or where you want to ensure immutability.

Example with Value Receiver

```go
func (r Rectangle) Perimeter() float64 {return 2 * (r.width + r.height)
}
```

In this method, calling `Perimeter` does not affect the original `Rectangle`, as `Perimeter` reads the values.### Pointer Receivers
Delegating a method to a pointer receiver allows the method to modify the original struct. When the receiveris a pointer, any changes made to its fields will affect the original instance.

Example with Pointer Receiver

```go
func (r *Rectangle) SetDimensions(width, height float64) {r.width = width
r.height = height
}
```

In this case, `SetDimensions` updates the original struct's fields. This method is useful when the goal is tochange the state of the object.

When to Use What?

Small Structs: For small structs (generally less than 16 bytes), prefer value receivers. They arelightweight, and the performance overhead of copying is usually negligible.

Large Structs: For larger structs, pointer receivers are preferred to avoid the cost and complexityassociated with copying.

Mutability: If your method modifies the receiver, use a pointer receiver. If your method only readsdata and does not need to modify the state, both value and pointer receivers are valid, but value receivers ensure immutability.

Consistency: In most cases, it's best to stick with one receiver type for a given type. If you choose pointer receivers for some methods, consistently use pointer receivers for all methods of that type.

Understanding methods and the difference between value and pointer receivers is fundamental for creating robust and efficient Go programs. Selecting the appropriate receiver type is key to managing the behavior ofyour types effectively. As you dive deeper into Go, mastering these concepts will enhance your ability to write clear, performant, and idiomatic code. In the following chapter, we will explore interfaces and polymorphism in Go and how methods interact with them to provide powerful design patterns.

Building Flexible Systems with Interfaces in Go

One of the most effective tools available to Go developers for achieving this flexibility is the concept of interfaces. By leveraging interfaces, developers can decouple components, promote code reuse, and make systems easier to test and extend. This chapter delves into the nature of interfaces in Go, their role in building flexible systems, and best practices for their implementation.

1. Understanding Interfaces in Go

In Go, an interface is a type that defines a contract for behavior. It specifies a set of method signatures, but does not provide implementations for these methods. Any type that implements these methods satisfies the interface, thereby allowing for polymorphism. This means you can write code that operates on interfaces rather than concrete types, which enhances flexibility.

1.1 Creating an Interface

To define an interface in Go, we use the `type` keyword followed by the name of the interface and its method signatures. Here's an example of a simple `Shape` interface:

```go
type Shape interface {Area() float64 Perimeter() float64
}
```

1.2 Implementing an Interface

Any type can implement an interface simply by providing the methods defined in the interface. There's no explicit declaration of intent to implement an interface, which is in line with Go's design philosophy of simplicity. Here's how you could implement the `Shape` interface with a `Circle` type:

```go
type Circle struct {Radius float64
}

func (c Circle) Area() float64 {
return math.Pi * c.Radius * c.Radius
}

func (c Circle) Perimeter() float64 {return 2 * math.Pi *
c.Radius
}
```

Similarly, you can create a `Rectangle` type:

```go
type Rectangle struct {Width float64

Height float64
}

func (r Rectangle) Area() float64 { return r.Width *
r.Height
```

```
}

func (r Rectangle) Perimeter() float64 {return 2 * (r.Width
+ r.Height)
}
```

2. Benefits of Using Interfaces ### 2.1 Decoupling Components
When components depend on interfaces rather than concrete types, they become more decoupled. This means you can change the implementation of a type without affecting any code that uses the interface. For example, if we need to add a new shape, like `Triangle`, we just implement the `Shape` interface without modifying any existing code that utilizes `Shape`.

2.2 Code Reusability

Interfaces promote code reusability by allowing you to develop flexible functions that can operate on multiple types. For instance, you can create a function that takes a `Shape` as an argument:

```go
func PrintShapeInfo(s Shape) {
fmt.Printf("Area:   %v,   Perimeter:   %v\n",   s.Area(),
s.Perimeter())
}
```

This function can accept any type that implements the `Shape` interface, such as `Circle` or `Rectangle`. ###

107

2.3 Testing and Mocking

Interfaces also facilitate unit testing. By using interfaces, you can easily create mock implementations to test your code's behavior in isolation. Consider a scenario where you have a function that relies on a logging service. You can create a mock logger that implements the logger interface solely for testing purposes.

```go
type Logger interface {Log(message string)
}

type MockLogger struct {messages []string
}

func (m *MockLogger) Log(message string) { m.messages
= append(m.messages, message)
}

// Example function that uses a Loggerfunc ProcessData(l
Logger) {
l.Log("Processing started.")
// Processing logic l.Log("Processing finished.")
}
```

3. Design Patterns Leveraging Interfaces

Go's interfaces play a crucial role in various design patterns that aid in building flexible systems. Below are a few patterns that utilize interfaces effectively.

3.1 Strategy Pattern

The Strategy pattern defines a family of algorithms, encapsulates each algorithm, and makes them interchangeable. In Go, you can define an interface representing an algorithm and different struct types implementing this interface.

```go
type SortStrategy interface {Sort([]int) []int
}

type BubbleSort struct{}
func (b BubbleSort) Sort(data []int) []int {
// Bubble sort implementationreturn data // Placeholder
}

type QuickSort struct{}
func (q QuickSort) Sort(data []int) []int {
// Quick sort implementationreturn data // Placeholder
}

type Context struct { strategy SortStrategy
}

func (c *Context) SetStrategy(s SortStrategy) {c.strategy =
s
}

func (c *Context) SortData(data []int) []int { return
c.strategy.Sort(data)
}
```

3.2 Observer Pattern

The Observer pattern allows a subject to notify multiple observers about changes in its state. In Go, this can be implemented using an interface for observers.

```go
type Observer interface {Update(data string)
}

type Subject struct { observers []Observer
}

func (s *Subject) RegisterObserver(o Observer) {
s.observers = append(s.observers, o)
}

func (s *Subject) NotifyObservers(data string) { for _,
observer := range s.observers {
observer.Update(data)
}
}
```

4. Best Practices for Interfaces

While interfaces provide powerful capabilities, use them wisely. Here are some best practices to guide you: ### 4.1 Keep Interfaces Small
Prefer small, focused interfaces that serve a single purpose. This promotes adherence to the Interface Segregation Principle and makes implementations easier to manage and test.

4.2 Use Meaningful Names

Choose descriptive names that convey the purpose of the interface. For instance, `Shape`, `Logger`, and `SortStrategy` all indicate their functionality clearly. ### 4.3 Avoid Interface Emission
Where possible, avoid creating interfaces just to satisfy a particular requirement. Use interfaces when you have multiple implementations or anticipate future variability.

4.4 Favor Composition over Inheritance

Go emphasizes composition over inheritance. Use interfaces to compose functionalities instead of directly inheriting traits from base types.

Interfaces are a cornerstone of building flexible and maintainable systems in Go. They enable developers to decouple components, enhance code reusability, and facilitate easier testing. By understanding how to effectively utilize interfaces, you can design systems that evolve gracefully over time, accommodate new requirements seamlessly, and remain robust against changes. As you continue your journey in Go programming, embrace interfaces as a powerful tool in your development arsenal.

Chapter 7: Embracing Concurrent Programming

With the rise of multicore processors and distributed computing systems, embracing concurrent programming has become not just an option but a necessity for developers aiming to create high- performance software. This chapter will delve into the principles, techniques, and tools necessary for integrating concurrency into your programming practices, ultimately empowering you to build robust andscalable applications.

Understanding Concurrency

At its core, concurrency refers to the ability of a program to handle multiple tasks simultaneously or in overlapping time frames. Unlike parallelism, which involves executing multiple tasks at the same time on multiple processors, concurrency emphasizes the structure and design of systems that allow multiple operations to occur together. Understanding these concepts is fundamental as we explore various programming models and structures.

Why Concurrency?

The advantages of concurrency are manifold:

Improved Performance: By utilizing multiple cores, concurrent programming can lead to significant performance gains, particularly for compute-intensive applications.

Responsiveness: For applications with a user interface, concurrency allows the program to remain responsive to user inputs while processing background tasks.

Resource Sharing: Concurrency facilitates better resource utilization by allowing multiple processes or threads to share resources like memory, files, and network connections.

Simplified Problem-Solving: Many real-world problems can be modeled as concurrent processes,making it easier to devise solutions that mirror their complexity.

The Building Blocks of Concurrent Programming

To get started with concurrent programming, it's essential to understand its fundamental constructs. This includes threads, processes, and synchronization mechanisms.

Threads vs. Processes

Processes are independent execution units that have their own memory space. Communication between processes is typically more complex due to the isolation between them.

Threads, on the other hand, are lightweight units of execution that run within a shared memory space of a process. Threads can share data more efficiently, but they require careful management to avoid conflicts.

Synchronization

When multiple threads or processes operate in a shared environment, synchronization becomes crucial to prevent data corruption and ensure consistent results. Several synchronization techniques include:

Mutexes: Short for mutual exclusions, mutexes ensure that only one thread can access a resource at a time.

Semaphores: These are signaling mechanisms that control access to a common resource by multiple threads, allowing a set number of threads to execute simultaneously.

Condition Variables: These provide a way for threads to pause execution until a certain condition is met, enabling efficient resource management.

Asynchronous Programming

In addition to traditional concurrency models, asynchronous programming offers an alternative paradigm that can simplify the execution of concurrent tasks. Async/await patterns, commonly found in languages like JavaScript and Python, allow developers to write non-blocking code that resembles synchronous flow. This style lets you handle multiple operations without the complexity of thread management, making it attractive for I/O-bound applications.

Tools and Frameworks

With a solid understanding of concurrency, the next step is to explore the tools and frameworks available to streamline concurrent programming. Here's a look at some prominent options:

Programming Languages

Java: With built-in concurrency support, the Java platform provides robust libraries such as the java.util.concurrent package that simplifies multithreading.

Go: Designed with concurrency in mind, Go uses goroutines and channels to manage concurrent execution and data exchange easily.

Rust: Emphasizing safety, Rust's ownership model ensures that data races are minimized, allowing developers to write concurrent code confidently.

Frameworks

Akka: Built on the actor model, Akka enables developers to create concurrent and distributed applications in Scala and Java, focusing on scalability and resilience.

ReactiveX: This library allows for asynchronous programming through observable sequences, promoting a functional style of programming across various languages.

Best Practices for Concurrent Programming

When embarking on a journey into concurrent programming, certain best practices can help ensure successand maintainability:

Reduce Shared State: Minimize the use of shared data between threads whenever possible to limit the potential for data races and make synchronization easier.

Use High-Level Abstractions: Leverage existing libraries and frameworks that provide abstractions for concurrency, allowing you to avoid the pitfalls of low-level thread management.

Test Concurrent Codes Rigorously: Concurrency introduces a layer of complexity that can lead to subtle bugs. Implement comprehensive testing strategies that account for race conditions and deadlocks.

Monitor Performance: Utilize profiling tools to understand the behavior of your concurrent system, identifying bottlenecks and optimizing performance.

Embracing concurrent programming is essential in today's software development environment. As we've explored in this chapter, understanding the principles, using effective tools, and adhering to best practices can empower developers to build applications that are not only faster and more efficient but also capable ofhandling the complexities of modern workloads. As you continue to refine your skills in concurrent programming, remember that learning is an ongoing journey—one that opens doors to new challenges and immense opportunities in the world of technology.

Goroutines: Lightweight Concurrency in Action

At the heart of Go's concurrency model is the concept of goroutines — a powerful, yet lightweight mechanism that allows developers to run functions concurrently without the overhead often associated withtraditional threads.

Understanding Goroutines

Goroutines are functions that run concurrently with other functions. A goroutine is simply a function declared with the `go` keyword before its invocation, and the Go runtime manages the execution of these goroutines. This lightweight model allows thousands (or even millions) of goroutines to execute simultaneously, drastically reducing the resource consumption compared to operating system threads.

When you invoke a function as a goroutine, it is executed independently of the rest of your program. This means that the main function continues executing, while the goroutine handles other tasks in the background. Here's a simple example to illustrate how to start a goroutine:

```go
package main

import ("fmt"
"time"
)
```

```
func sayHello() {
fmt.Println("Hello from goroutine!")
}

func main() {
go sayHello() // Start sayHello() as a goroutine

// Sleep for a short period to allow goroutine to finish
time.Sleep(1 * time.Second)
fmt.Println("Back in main function!")
}
```

In this example, calling `go sayHello()` starts the `sayHello` function in a new goroutine. The main function will print its message after a short sleep to ensure that the goroutine has time to execute. Without the sleep, it's possible that the main function would finish executing before the goroutine has had a chance to run.

The Cost of Concurrency

Goroutines are designed to be lightweight; the Go runtime uses a small fixed-size stack that grows and shrinks automatically as needed. This efficiency allows a single OS thread to manage multiple goroutines, thus minimizing context switching overhead and enhancing performance. In contrast, traditional threads can consume a significant amount of memory and resources, making scaling cumbersome.

As an illustration, you can create a large number of goroutines in Go:

118

```go
func main() {
for i := 0; i < 100000; i++ {
go func(n int) { fmt.Println(n)
}(i)
}

// Sleep to ensure all goroutines complete before main
exitstime.Sleep(5 * time.Second)
}
```

In the example above, we spawn 100,000 goroutines, each printing its own index. The Go runtime effectively manages these goroutines, showcasing how scaling concurrency with goroutines is manageableand efficient.

Synchronization and Coordination

Even though goroutines make it easier to run tasks concurrently, coordinating and synchronizing their execution is crucial in concurrent programming. Go provides various synchronization primitives through the `sync` package, enabling developers to prevent race conditions and inconsistent states.

One of the most common synchronization tools is the WaitGroup, which allows you to wait for a collection of goroutines to finish executing:

```go
package main
```

```go
import ("fmt"
"sync"
"time"
)

func worker(id int, wg *sync.WaitGroup) {
defer wg.Done() // Notify that this goroutine is done
time.Sleep(time.Second)        //      Simulate      work
fmt.Printf("Worker %d finished\n", id)
}

func main() {
var wg sync.WaitGroup

for i := 1; i <= 5; i++ {
wg.Add(1)  //  Increment  the  WaitGroup  counter  go
worker(i, &wg)
}

wg.Wait()  //  Block  until  all  goroutines  finished
fmt.Println("All workers completed.")
}
```

In the above code, the `worker` function simulates a task by sleeping for a second, and when it finishes, it calls `wg.Done()` to let the `WaitGroup` know that the goroutine has completed. The `main` function adds five goroutines to the `WaitGroup`, and after starting them, it waits for their completion with `wg.Wait()`.

Channels: Communicating Between Goroutines

Goroutines can communicate with each other using channels, a powerful feature that allows you to safelysend data between concurrent tasks. Channels act as conduits through which goroutines can exchange information. Here's a simple demonstration:

```go
package main

import ("fmt"
)

func sum(a []int, resultChan chan int) {sum := 0
for _, v := range a {sum += v
}
resultChan <- sum // Send sum to channel
}

func main() {
numbers := []int{1, 2, 3, 4, 5} resultChan := make(chan int)

go sum(numbers, resultChan)

result := <-resultChan // Receive from channel
fmt.Printf("The sum is: %d\n", result)
}
```

In this example, the `sum` function calculates the sum of an integer slice and sends the result back through a channel. The main function receives the result from the channel, demonstrating how goroutines can communicate safely without explicit locking mechanisms.

Goroutines are indeed a landmark feature of the Go programming language, embodying the concept of lightweight concurrency in action. Their simplicity, efficiency, and the accompanying tools provided by Go's standard library make them a solid choice for developers looking to implement concurrent systems. Whether you're building web servers, network applications, or command-line tools, understanding and mastering goroutines can greatly enhance the performance and responsiveness of your applications.

As you delve deeper into Go's concurrency model, you will discover new capabilities and patterns that enable you to manage complexity and build robust applications. The power of goroutines is not just in their ability to run concurrently but also in how they promote clear, maintainable code through their integration with channels and synchronization tools. Embrace concurrency with Go, and watch your applications flourish in a world that demands efficient execution.

Synchronization and Communication with Channels

This chapter explores the concept of channels as a mechanism for synchronization and communication in concurrent programming. We will cover the fundamentals of channels, their implementation in different programming paradigms, and best practices for their effective use.

Understanding Concurrency

Concurrent programming refers to the ability of a system to handle multiple tasks simultaneously. This can be achieved through various methods such as multi-threading, asynchronous programming, or distributed computing. A typical use case for concurrency involves an application that needs to perform I/O operations, such as reading from a file or retrieving data from a network, while still being responsive to user interactions.

Challenges of Concurrent Programming

While concurrency offers advantages, it also introduces challenges such as race conditions, deadlocks, and difficulty in debugging. Race conditions occur when two or more threads attempt to modify shared data simultaneously, leading to unpredictable results. Deadlocks happen when two or more threads are waiting for each other to release resources, resulting in a standstill. To overcome these challenges, effective synchronization mechanisms are essential.

Channels: An Overview

Channels are a powerful abstraction for communication between concurrent processes. By providing a straightforward way to send and receive messages, channels facilitate synchronization, making it easier to coordinate actions between threads or processes. Unlike traditional locks and shared memory access, channels encourage a more structured communication model, reducing the risk of common concurrency issues.

Features of Channels

Message Passing: Channels enable processes to exchange messages without necessarily sharing memory. This decouples the sender and receiver, making the system more modular.

Synchronization: Channels can implicitly synchronize the flow of control. When a process sends a message through a channel, it may block until the message is received, ensuring that data is sent and received in the correct order and at the right time.

Buffering: Channels can be either buffered or unbuffered. Unbuffered channels require the sender and receiver to synchronize explicitly, while buffered channels allow for some level of decoupling by providing a storage capacity for messages.

Type Safety: In many programming languages, channels can enforce type safety. This prevents type-related errors by ensuring that only compatible types are exchanged between processes.

Implementing Channels in Various Programming Languages### Go

The Go programming language is renowned for its built-in support for concurrency through goroutines andchannels. In Go, a channel can be created using the `make` function, providing an easy way to send and receive data.

```go
package main

import ("fmt"
)

func main() {
// Create a channel
messages := make(chan string)

// Goroutine to send messagesgo func() {
messages <- "Hello, World!"
}()

// Receive messagemsg := <-messagesfmt.Println(msg)
}
```

In this example, a goroutine is spawned to send a message to the channel. The main function then waits for this message, demonstrating basic communication and synchronization.

Rust

In Rust, channels are part of the standard library (`std::sync::mpsc`). Rust's ownership model and thread safety features ensure that data sent through channels avoids common pitfalls found in other languages.

```rust
```

```rust
use std::sync::mpsc;use std::thread;

fn main() {
let (tx, rx) = mpsc::channel();

thread::spawn(move || { tx.send("Hello, Rust!").unwrap();
});

let msg = rx.recv().unwrap();println!("{}", msg);
}
```
```

Rust's compile-time checks and ownership system provide strong guarantees that the data is safely sent and received across threads.

### Python

Python offers several libraries for concurrent programming, including the `queue` module, which allows for safe communication and synchronization between threads.

```python import threadingimport queue

def worker(q):
q.put("Hello, Python!")

q = queue.Queue()
thread = threading.Thread(target=worker, args=(q,))
thread.start()

msg = q.get()print(msg)
```
```

```
```

In this Python example, a thread is created to send a message through a queue, which serves as a channel for communication.

Best Practices for Using Channels

Limit Shared State: Whenever possible, limit the use of shared states between processes. Channels provide a natural mechanism for data exchange, reducing the need for shared memory.

Error Handling: Be vigilant about error handling, especially when receiving messages through channels. Incorporate checks to handle potential issues such as closed channels or message parsing errors.

Choose the Right Channel Type: Assess your use case before choosing between buffered and unbuffered channels. Buffered channels can help when you need to decouple senders and receivers, whileunbuffered channels are useful for strict synchronization.

Profiling and Performance: Monitor the performance of your channel-based architecture. Profile your application to identify bottlenecks and understand the impact of concurrency on overall performance.

Channels represent a robust method for achieving synchronization and communication in concurrent programming. By leveraging message passing rather than shared memory, channels minimize the complications associated with traditional concurrency mechanisms. As developers embrace modern programming paradigms, understanding and effectively utilizing channels will be critical in building scalable, responsive, and reliable applications. Through careful implementation and adherence to best practices, channels can significantly enhance the efficiency and maintainability of concurrent systems.

Chapter 8: Utilizing Go Packages

In this chapter, we will explore the powerful concept of packages in the Go programming language (Golang). Packages serve as the primary means of organizing and managing code in Go, promoting code reuse, modularity, and collaboration. Understanding how to efficiently utilize Go packages can vastly improve your development workflow, making your programs more scalable and maintainable.

8.1 What Are Go Packages?

A Go package is essentially a collection of Go source files in a single directory that are compiled together. Each Go file in the package begins with a declaration of the package name. The package name typically represents the functionality of the contained files and is used to reference the package in other Go files.

8.1.1 Package Declaration

At the top of each Go source file, you will find the `package` declaration. For example, a file named `math.go` that contains mathematical functions would begin with the following line:

```go
package math
```

If you were to create another file in the same directory, it would also start with `package math`, indicating that all files belong to the same package.

8.1.2 The Package Structure

A Go package can contain multiple files, each potentially defining different functionalities but working together to fulfill a common purpose. The directory structure for Go packages is straightforward: each package resides in its own directory, and the directory name should match the package name for consistency.

For example, the following is a sample structure for a hypothetical package named `calculator`:

```
calculator/
add.go subtract.go multiply.godivide.go
```

8.2 Creating Your Own Package

To create your own Go package, follow these steps:

Create a Directory: Create a directory for your package.
Write Your Code: Inside this directory, create `.go` files to implement the functionalities of thepackage.
Declare the Package: Make sure to declare the package at the top of each file.
Export Functions: Functions that need to be accessible outside the package must start with an uppercase letter.

Here's an example of a simple package `mathutils`:

130

```go
// File: mathutils/add.gopackage mathutils

// Add two integers
func Add(a int, b int) int {return a + b
}
```

```go
// File: mathutils/subtract.gopackage mathutils

// Subtract two integers
func Subtract(a int, b int) int {return a - b
}
```

8.2.1 Building the Package

To use the `mathutils` package, navigate to the parent directory and run `go build mathutils`. This command compiles the package and makes it available for use in other Go programs.

8.3 Importing Go Packages

Once you have defined your package, you can use it by importing it in another Go file. To import a package, use the `import` statement. Here's how you can use the `mathutils` package in your main application:

```go
package main
```

```go
import ("fmt"
"path/to/your/mathutils" // Adjust the import path based
on your project structure
)

func main() {
sum := mathutils.Add(5, 3)
difference := mathutils.Subtract(10, 4)

fmt.Println("Sum:",      sum)     fmt.Println("Difference:",
difference)
}
```

8.3.1 Import Aliasing

If you find that the package name is long or clashes with an existing name, you can alias the import:

```go
import mu "path/to/your/mathutils"

func main() {
sum := mu.Add(5, 3)
...
}
```

8.4 Third-Party Packages

In addition to creating your own packages, Go has a vibrant ecosystem of third-party packages that you can integrate into your projects. The standard way to manage dependencies in Go is through Go modules.

8.4.1 Go Modules

To create a new module, navigate to your project directory and run:

```bash
go mod init myproject
```

This command will create a `go.mod` file that keeps track of your dependencies. To add a third-party package, such as the popular `gorilla/mux` for HTTP routing, you can run:

```bash
go get github.com/gorilla/mux
```

This command downloads the package and updates your `go.mod` file automatically. ## 8.5 Best Practices for Using Packages
8.5.1 Organize Your Code

Proper organization of your packages is crucial for scalability. Group related functionality together, and respect the single responsibility principle by ensuring each package has a clear focus.

8.5.2 Keep It Simple

Avoid overcomplicating your packages with unnecessary abstractions. The goal is to promote reusability and simplicity.

8.5.3 Document Your Packages

Use Go's documentation comments to explain the functionality of your package and its exported functions. This is invaluable for anyone who may use your package in the future, including yourself.

8.5.4 Regular Updates

If you rely on third-party packages, keep them updated regularly to benefit from the latest features and security patches. You can use `go get -u` to update your dependencies.

Utilizing Go packages effectively is pivotal for writing clean, maintainable, and modular code. By leveraging both your own packages and the extensive array of third-party packages available, you can significantly enhance your Go programming projects. Embrace packages as building blocks in your journey as a Go developer, and you'll find that they not only simplify your code but also accelerate yourdevelopment process.

Working with Standard Library Packages in Go

Go, also known as Golang, is a statically typed, compiled programming language designed for simplicity and efficiency. One of its most powerful features is its extensive standard library, which provides a rich set of packages for a variety of programming tasks—from file handling and string manipulation to network communication and concurrent programming. In this chapter, we will explore the essential standard library packages in Go, how to effectively use them, and practical examples that demonstrate their capabilities.

Understanding the Standard Library

The Go standard library is a collection of packages that provide reusable code for common tasks. These packages are included in the Go installation, eliminating the need for developers to download or manage external dependencies for many basic operations. The organization of the standard library is modular, allowing you to import only what you need for your project.

To access the standard library, you use the `import` statement in your Go programs. For example, to use the `fmt` package for formatted I/O, you would start your program like this:

```go
package main

import ("fmt"
)
```

Key Packages in the Standard Library

Here are some of the most commonly used packages in

the Go standard library:

fmt: For formatted I/O operations. It includes functions for formatting strings, printing output to the console, and reading input.

```go
fmt.Println("Hello, World!")
```

math: Provides basic constants and mathematical functions. It includes operations such as square roots, trigonometric functions, and logarithms.

```go
import "math"

result := math.Pow(2, 3) // 2 raised to the power of 3
```

strings: Contains functions for string manipulation, such as searching, replacing, and splitting strings.

```go
import "strings"

s := "hello,golang"
parts := strings.Split(s, ",") // splits on commas
```

time: Provides functionality for measuring and displaying time. It includes features for parsing and formatting dates and times.

```go
import "time"

now := time.Now()
fmt.Println("Current time:", now.Format(time.RFC1123))
```

net/http: Implements HTTP clients and servers. It's a powerhouse for web-related tasks, allowing you to build web servers and clients effortlessly.

```go
import (
"net/http""fmt"
)

func handler(w http.ResponseWriter, r *http.Request) {
fmt.Fprintf(w, "Hello, you've requested: %s\n", r.URL.Path)
}

func main() { http.HandleFunc("/", handler)
http.ListenAndServe(":8080", nil)
}
```

Importing Packages

To use a package, you import it at the beginning of your Go file. Multiple packages can be imported at once, which helps in organizing imports neatly. Here's an example:

```go
import (
```

```
"fmt"
"math" "strings"
)
```

When using packages, keep in mind that you should use the appropriate functions by referring to the package name, which helps avoid naming collisions. For example, if `math.Sqrt` is referenced, it's clear that the `Sqrt` function is coming from the `math` package.

Best Practices for Using Standard Library Packages

Understand the Package Documentation: Before using a package, a good practice is to read its documentation. Go has excellent documentation available online at pkg.go.dev, which

provides examples, explanations, and details about functions, types, and methods provided by each package.

Use Type Aliases Appropriately: Sometimes, the names in standard packages can be long or verbose. You can define an alias to simplify your code, but be cautious of readability.

```go
import (
httpClient "net/http"
)

resp, err := httpClient.Get("http://example.com")
```

Error Handling: Many functions in the Go standard library return errors. Always check for errors to ensure robust code.

```go
resp, err := http.Get("http://example.com")if err != nil {
log.Fatalf("Error fetching URL: %v", err)
}
```

Code Reusability: Use standard library functions and types to avoid reinventing the wheel. This helpskeep your code clean and maintainable.

Performance Considerations: The standard library is highly optimized, so prefer built-in functions fortasks like sorting, string operations, or networking, rather than writing custom implementations.

Advanced Packages

While the basic packages provide essential functionality, Go also offers more advanced ones, such as:

context: This package is used for managing deadlines, cancellation signals, and other request-scoped values across API boundaries and between processes.

sync: Offers basic synchronization primitives such as mutual exclusion locks, which are crucial in concurrent programming.

encoding/json: Provides functions for encoding and

decoding JSON, which is essential for web APIs and data interchange formats.

```go
import (
"encoding/json""fmt"
)

type Person struct {
Name string `json:"name"`Age  int        `json:"age"`
}

func main() {
p := Person{Name: "Alice", Age: 30} jsonData, _ :=
json.Marshal(p) fmt.Println(string(jsonData))
}
```

The Go standard library is one of the language's strongest aspects, providing a broad array of tools for building efficient and effective applications. By familiarizing yourself with the various packages and their functionalities, you can significantly speed up development while writing clean and maintainable code. Embrace the power of the standard library and make it an integral part of your Go programming journey!

Creating and Managing Custom Packages in Go

One of the key features that contribute to Go's effectiveness is its robust package management system. In this chapter, we will explore how to create and manage custom packages in Go, enabling you to encapsulate functionality in reusable modules.

1. Understanding Packages in Go

A package in Go is essentially a directory that contains Go source files. Each package can contain related code that can be used by itself or can be imported into other packages. Packages help in organizing code and avoiding name conflicts by grouping related functions, types, and variables under a unique name.

1.1 The Package Declaration

Each Go file must start with a `package` declaration. This declaration specifies the name of the package the file belongs to. For example:

```go
package mathutils
```

This declaration indicates that the file belongs to the `mathutils` package.### 1.2 Importing Packages
To use a package, you need to import it into your Go file. Importing packages allows you to access exported identifiers from other packages. An identifier is considered exported when it starts with a capital letter.

```go
import "fmt" import "mathutils"
```

1.3 The Go Module System

Before Go Modules were introduced in Go 1.11, dependency management was done using GOPATH, which had limitations. The introduction of modules has revolutionized how Go handles package dependencies.
Using modules, you can manage versions and dependencies more effectively.To create a new Go module, you can run:
```bash
go mod init your-module-name
```

This command creates a `go.mod` file in your project directory which will track your module'sdependencies.

2. Creating a Custom Package

Let's create a simple custom package as an example. We'll create a package named `mathutils` that provides some mathematical utility functions.

2.1 Directory Structure

First, set up your directory structure:

```
/project
/mathutils mathutils.go
main.go
```

2.2 Writing the Package Code

In `mathutils/mathutils.go`, define your package and add some functions:

```go
package mathutils

// Add returns the sum of two integers. func Add(a int, b int) int {
return a + b
}

// Subtract returns the difference of two integers. func Subtract(a int, b int) int {
return a - b
}
```

2.3 Creating the Main Application

Now let's use the `mathutils` package in your `main.go` file.

```go
package main

import ("fmt"
"project/mathutils"
)

func main() {
sum := mathutils.Add(5, 3) diff := mathutils.Subtract(5, 3)

fmt.Println("Sum:", sum) fmt.Println("Difference:", diff)
```

```
}
```

To run the application, navigate to the `project` directory and execute:

```bash
go run main.go
```

You should see:

```
Sum: 8
Difference: 2
```

3. Managing Dependencies

One of the key capabilities of Go modules is managing dependencies effectively. As you develop your application, you might want to use third-party packages. You can add these dependencies using:

```bash
go get github.com/some/dependency
```

The `go.mod` file will automatically update to include the new dependency along with its version. ### 3.1 Updating Dependencies
To update a package to its latest version, you can run:

```bash
```

```bash
go get -u github.com/some/dependency
```

3.2 Tidying Up Dependencies

After adding or removing dependencies, it's good practice to tidy up your module with:

```bash
go mod tidy
```

This command removes unnecessary dependencies and adds any missing ones.## 4. Versioning and Tagging
Versioning your own packages is also essential, especially if you plan to share them publicly. When you have significant updates to your package, consider tagging a version:

```bash
git tag v1.0.0
git push origin v1.0.0
```

Then, other users can specify the version in their `go.mod` file like so:

```go
require github.com/yourusername/yourpackage v1.0.0
```

5. Best Practices for Custom Packages

Keep Packages Focused: Each package should have a single responsibility. This makes it easier to maintain and reuse.

Name Conventions: Use meaningful names for packages and keep them lowercase.

Documentation: Use comments to document the functionality of your package and each exported function.

Testing: Write tests for your custom packages to ensure functionality. Go has built-in support for testing with the `testing` package.

Creating and managing custom packages in Go is a fundamental skill that promotes code reusability and maintainability. By understanding how to structure your packages, manage dependencies, and follow best practices, you can build efficient and scalable applications in Go. As you delve deeper into Go development, you will find that effective package management will greatly enhance your productivity and the quality of your code.

Chapter 9: Testing and Debugging in Go

Writing reliable, maintainable, and bug-free code is not only essential for the integrity of a project but also for the peace of mind of developers. In this chapter, we will explore the built-in testing features of the Go programming language, different approaches to debugging, and best practices that can enhance your development workflow.

9.1 Introduction to Testing in Go

Go has a rich testing package that supports both unit testing and benchmark testing. The `testing` package provides developers with the tools they need to create effective tests. This functionality is part of the standard library, making it readily accessible for all Go developers without the need for external libraries.

9.1.1 Writing Tests

To get started, let's see how to create a simple test. Before writing tests, it's essential to understand the Go convention for file naming: test files must end with `_test.go`. Here's a quick example demonstrating how we can create a function and a corresponding test for it.

```go
// math.go - a simple math packagepackage math

// Add takes two integers and returns their sum. func Add(a, b int) int {
return a + b
```

```
}
```

Now, let's write a test for the `Add` function:

```go
// math_test.gopackage math

import "testing"

func TestAdd(t *testing.T) {result := Add(2, 3) expected :=
5

if result != expected {
t.Errorf("Add(2, 3) = %d; want %d", result, expected)
}
}
```

9.1.2 Running Tests

To execute the tests, execute the following command in the terminal:

```bash
go test
```

Go will automatically find any test functions (those that start with `Test`) and run them. The `go test` tool summarizes the results, indicating which tests passed and which failed.

9.1.3 Testing for Errors

In many applications, especially those that deal with I/O operations or external data, handling errors is crucial. Here's how to test for expected errors:

```go
// divide.go - a simple divide functionpackage math

import ( "errors"
)

// Divide takes two integers and returns the quotient and an error if the divisor is zero. func Divide(a, b int) (int, error) {
if b == 0 {
return 0, errors.New("division by zero")
}
return a / b, nil
}
```

The corresponding test for the `Divide` function could look like this:

```go
// divide_test.gopackage math

import "testing"

func TestDivide(t *testing.T) {
_, err := Divide(10, 0)if err == nil {
t.Error("Expected an error but got none")
}

result, err := Divide(10, 2)expected := 5
if result != expected {
t.Errorf("Divide(10, 2) = %d; want %d", result, expected)
}
}
```

9.1.4 Benchmarking

In addition to regular tests, Go provides support for benchmarking. This is beneficial for identifying performance bottlenecks in your code. Here's how you can create a benchmark test:

```go
// math_test.gopackage math

import "testing"

func BenchmarkAdd(b *testing.B) {for i := 0; i < b.N; i++
{
Add(2, 3)
}
```

```
}
```

To run the benchmarks, use the command:

```bash
go test -bench=.
```

This command runs all tests and benchmarks in the current package, providing insights into the performance of your functions.

9.2 Debugging in Go

While testing aims to prevent bugs, debugging assists in resolving them when they arise. Go provides several tools and methodologies for effective debugging.

9.2.1 Using Print Statements

Sometimes, the simplest way to see what's happening in your code is by adding print statements. Using `fmt.Println()` or `log.Println()` can help trace issues during development. However, be mindful that overusing print statements can clutter the output and make it harder to find relevant information.

9.2.2 The Go Debugger (delve)

The Go community has a powerful debugger called `delve`. It allows developers to step through their programs, inspect variables, and evaluate expressions interactively. To install delve, you can run:

```bash
go install github.com/go-delve/delve/cmd/dlv@latest
```

Once installed, you can run your program in debug mode:

```bash
dlv debug your_program.go
```

Delve provides a command-line interface to set breakpoints, watch variables, and evaluate expressions on the fly.

9.2.3 Error Handling and Reporting

Consistent error handling is vital in any Go application. Use Go's `error` type to capture and handle errors gracefully. Additionally, creating custom error types can provide more context-specific information, improving debugging efforts when things go wrong.

9.2.4 Logging

In production code, utilizing a logging framework is essential for diagnosing issues. Go's standard library provides the `log` package. You can create structured logs with levels such as debug, info, warning, and error. Here's a basic example:

```go
import (
```

```
"log"
"os"
)

func init() { log.SetOutput(os.Stdout)
log.SetFlags(log.LstdFlags | log.Lshortfile)
}

// Example Functionfunc example() {
log.Println("This is an informational log message.")
}
```
` ` `

9.3 Best Practices for Testing and Debugging

To ensure a seamless testing and debugging experience, consider adopting the following best practices: ### 9.3.1 Write Tests Early and Often
Integrate testing into your development process. Implement tests as you go, especially before releasing new features or making changes. This reduces the likelihood of bugs and eases refactoring.

9.3.2 Use Table-Driven Tests

Table-driven tests are a Go idiom where you define a series of input/output pairs and iterate through them in your test function. This approach keeps your tests concise and easy to extend.

9.3.3 Isolate Tests from External Dependencies

Use mocking to isolate tests from external dependencies

153

like databases or APIs. This helps ensure that unit tests can run quickly and consistently on any machine.

9.3.4 Apply Good Error Handling

Adopt a consistent error handling strategy. Always check errors returned from functions and handle them appropriately. Good practices include returning informative error messages and not ignoring errors.

9.3.5 Make Use of Assertions

Although Go's testing package does not have built-in assertion functions, libraries like `stretchr/testify` can enhance the readability of tests. Using assertions can simplify failure messages and improve test clarity.

In this chapter, we have delved into the testing and debugging capabilities of Go. By leveraging Go's robust testing framework, utilizing effective debugging tools like `delve`, and adhering to best practices, developers can create reliable applications that are easier to maintain and debug.

Testing and debugging are not just tasks to check off; they are vital skills that will contribute to the overall success of your projects and enhance your abilities as a Go developer. As you continue your programming journey, embrace these practices and tools, and you'll find that they pay dividends in the quality of your code and your development experience.

Writing Unit Tests with Go's Testing Framework

By executing functions in isolation, developers can identify defects early, improve code quality, and facilitate future changes. Go, also known as Golang, is a statically typed, compiled programming language developed at Google. It provides a robust and straightforward testing framework that encourages good testing practices. In this chapter, we will explore the philosophy behind unit testing in Go, how to write and execute tests, and best practices to maximize the effectiveness of your tests.

The Philosophy of Unit Testing in Go

In Go, testing is seen not only as a quality assurance measure but as an integral part of the development process. This philosophy is encapsulated in the saying, "test as you go." The Go community emphasizes that writing tests should be a seamless part of the coding workflow rather than an afterthought. As the language itself promotes simplicity and clarity, it ensures that writing tests is just as straightforward.

Why Unit Tests Matter

Confidence in Code Changes: Unit tests provide a safety net that helps you change your code withoutfear of introducing bugs. Running the tests assures you that existing functionality remains intact.

Clear Documentation: Well-written tests serve as documentation. They illustrate how functions areexpected to behave, making it easier for others (or yourself in the future) to understand the code.

Better Design: Writing tests often exposes poor design decisions, as it requires thinking about the interfaces and interactions between components.

Faster Debugging: When a test fails, you know exactly which component needs fixing, making debugging quicker and more efficient.

Setting Up the Testing Environment

Go's testing framework is built into the standard library, making it incredibly easy to get started. To demonstrate unit testing, let's assume we have a Go project folder structured as follows:

```
/my-go-projectmain.go mypackage
mypackage.go mypackage_test.go
```

The Test File Naming Convention

In Go, test files must end with `_test.go`. For example, if you are testing a package named `mypackage`, your test file should be named `mypackage_test.go`. This convention allows Go's tooling to identify the test files easily.

Writing Your First Unit Test

Let's create a sample package within `mypackage`. Suppose we have a file `mypackage.go` with a simple function:

```go
// mypackage.go package mypackage

// Add returns the sum of two integers.func Add(a, b int) int {
return a + b
}
```

Now, we will write a test for the `Add` function in `mypackage_test.go`:

```go
// mypackage_test.gopackage mypackage

import "testing"

// TestAdd is a test function for the Add function. func TestAdd(t *testing.T) {
result := Add(2, 3)expected := 5

if result != expected {
t.Errorf("Add(2, 3) = %d; want %d", result, expected)
}
}
```

Understanding the Test Function In the above example:

We import the `testing` package, which provides the necessary tools to create tests in Go.
Test functions must start with the word `Test` and take a pointer to `testing.T` as a parameter.
Inside the test, you can call the function you want to test and check if the result matches the expected value.
The `t.Errorf` method reports an error if the test fails, formatting the output to include useful debugging information.

Running Tests

To run the tests, navigate to the directory containing your Go files and use the following command:

```bash
go test
```

Go will automatically find all the files ending with `_test.go` in the current directory and execute the tests defined within. If all tests pass, you will see output indicating success. If a test fails, Go will provide helpful output detailing what went wrong.

Advanced Testing Techniques
Table-Driven Tests
Go developers often use a table-driven test pattern to test multiple scenarios with minimal code duplication. This technique is effective for testing functions that need to handle various inputs and expected outputs.
Here's how you could refactor our `TestAdd` function using a table-driven approach:

```go
```

```go
func TestAdd(t *testing.T) {cases := []struct {
a, b    int expected int
}{
{2, 3, 5},
{1, 1, 2},
{-1, -1, -2},
{0, 5, 5},
}

for _, c := range cases { result := Add(c.a, c.b) if result !=
c.expected {
t.Errorf("Add(%d, %d) = %d; want %d", c.a, c.b, result,
c.expected)
}
}
}
```

Benchmark Tests

In addition to standard unit tests, Go's testing framework allows you to write benchmark tests to measure the performance of your code. You can create a benchmark function by following this pattern:

```go
func BenchmarkAdd(b *testing.B) {for i := 0; i < b.N; i++
{
Add(1, 2)
}
}
```

To run benchmarks, use the command:

```bash
go test -bench=.
```

This will execute all benchmarks in your test files. ### Writing Integration Tests
While unit tests focus on individual components, integration tests check if different parts of your application work together correctly. Go's testing tools can be used in similar fashion for integration testing by composing tests that examine multiple components in your application. ## Best Practices for Writing Tests
Keep Tests Independent: Each test should be able to run in isolation. Don't let them rely on the outcome of other tests.

Test Only One Thing: Each test should assert one condition, improving clarity and making it easier to identify failures.

Descriptive Naming: Use clear and descriptive names for your tests to indicate what behavior isbeing tested.

Use Comments Wisely: Prefer self-documenting code through clear test cases over excessivecomments.

Run Tests Frequently: Make it a habit to run your tests after every change to ensure ongoing quality.

Focus on Edge Cases: Test not just typical scenarios but also edge cases to ensure your code behaves as expected under less common conditions.

Go's built-in testing framework is powerful yet approachable, making it easy for developers to integrate testing into their workflow. By adhering to best practices and leveraging the features provided by the Go testing framework, you can build robust applications with the confidence that your code is functioning as intended. As you continue your journey in Go, remember that testing is not just a task; it is an investment in the longevity and reliability of your code. Start testing early and often, and you will reap the benefits of a well-tested application.

Debugging Techniques for Efficient Problem-Solving in GO

This chapter explores various debugging techniques and tools that can enhance your problem-solving capabilities when developing in Go. From understanding basic debugging methods to utilizing advanced profiling and tracing tools, this chapter provides a comprehensive overview of how to effectively diagnose and resolve issues in Go applications.

1. Understanding Common Errors in Go

Before diving into specific debugging techniques, it's essential to understand the common types of errors one might encounter in Go. These include:

Compile-Time Errors: These errors occur during the compilation phase and often involve syntax mistakes, incorrect types, or unresolved references.

Runtime Errors: Runtime errors are encountered when the program is executed, typically causing panics. Common examples are division by zero, nil pointer dereferences, and array index out of bounds.

Logical Errors: These errors result in the program behaving incorrectly without producing explicit error messages. Logical errors can be tricky, as the program runs successfully but does not provide the expected results.

Understanding these error types not only aids in identifying issues but also helps to strategize the debuggingprocess effectively.

2. Basic Debugging Techniques ### 2.1 Print Statements

One of the most straightforward and traditional debugging techniques is the use of print statements. In Go, the `fmt.Println()` function can be used to output variable values and program execution states at various points in the code. While simple, this method can quickly provide insights into the flow of execution and help identify unexpected values.

Example:

```go
package mainimport "fmt"
func add(a, b int) int {
fmt.Println("Adding:", a, b) // Debugging outputreturn a + b
}
```

```go
func main() {
result := add(5, 10) fmt.Println("Result:", result)
}
```

2.2 Error Handling

Go encourages explicit error handling. By using the idiomatic error check (`if err != nil`) pattern, you can identify and manage errors effectively. This technique is essential for debugging since many issues arise from overlooked errors.

Example:

```go
package main

import ("fmt"
"os"
)

func main() {
file, err := os.Open("nonexistent.txt")if err != nil {
fmt.Println("Error opening file:", err) // Debugging outputreturn
}
defer file.Close()
}
```

3. Using the Go Debugger (`delve`)

For more advanced debugging needs, the Go community widely uses `delve`, an interactive debugger tailored for the Go programming language. With `delve`, developers can set breakpoints, step through code, inspect variables, and evaluate expressions dynamically.

3.1 Installing Delve

To install `delve`, use the following command:

```bash
go get -u github.com/go-delve/delve/cmd/dlv
```

3.2 Basic Commands

When executing `delve`, you can use various commands to facilitate your debugging:

`break [line number]`: Sets a breakpoint at the specified line.
`next`: Moves to the next line, skipping over function calls.
`step`: Steps into the function for deeper inspection.
`continue`: Resumes execution until the next breakpoint.
`print [variable]`: Displays the value of a variable.

Example of Using Delve:

```bash
dlv debug myapp.go
```

```
```

Once in the debugger, set a breakpoint and begin stepping through the code to monitor its state. ### 3.3 Using Watches

Delve allows you to set "watches" on variables, enabling inspection of their values every time the programstops at a breakpoint. This can be particularly useful for understanding how data changes over time in a complex application.

4. Profiling and Performance Analysis

Go's standard library includes powerful profiling tools that can help identify performance bottlenecks. The `net/http/pprof` package offers a convenient way to include profiling capabilities in your applications. ### 4.1 Integrating Pprof

To integrate `pprof`, import the package and start the pprof server:

```go
import (
_ "net/http/pprof""net/http"
)

func main() {go func() {
log.Println(http.ListenAndServe("localhost:8080", nil))
}()
}
```

4.2 Analyzing Performance

Once the server is running, you can analyze your application with tools like the `go tool pprof` command. This allows you to gather heap profiles, goroutine analyses, and CPU statistics, which are invaluable for optimizing performance.

Effective debugging is crucial for delivering high-quality Go applications. By mastering the basic techniquesof print statements and error handling, paired with sophisticated tools like delve and pprof, developers can significantly enhance their problem-solving efficiency.

Conclusion

As we reach the end of "Go Programming for Beginners: Master Go from Scratch with Easy-to-Follow Steps," we hope this journey through the fundamentals of Go has been both enlightening and empowering. You have taken the first steps into the world of programming with Go, a language that is renowned for its performance, simplicity, and efficiency in building reliable software.

Throughout this book, we have explored key concepts such as Go's syntax, data types, control structures, and concurrency. By breaking down these topics into manageable sections, we've aimed to provide you with a solid foundation that you can build upon as you continue to learn and grow your programming skills.

Remember, programming is a continuous learning process. The more you practice and experiment with the language, the more proficient you will become. Don't hesitate to dive into real-world projects, contribute to open-source, or engage with the vibrant Go community. Each of these experiences will deepen your understanding and enhance your capabilities as a programmer.

As you move forward, keep in mind the core principles of Go: simplicity, clarity, and efficiency. Allow these principles to guide your coding practices, and you'll find that developing robust applications becomes an enjoyable and rewarding endeavor.

Thank you for embarking on this journey with us. We are excited about the potential that lies ahead for you as you master Go and leverage its power to create remarkable software. Happy coding!

Biography

Tommy Clark is a passionate and dynamic author who combines a deep love for technology with an insatiable curiosity for innovation. As the mastermind behind the book *"Clark: A Journey Through Expertise and Innovation,"* Tommy brings years of hands-on experience in web development, web applications, and system administration to the forefront, offering readers a unique and insightful perspective.

With a strong background in Go programming and an ever-evolving fascination with crafting robust, efficient systems, Tommy excels at turning complex technical concepts into practical, actionable strategies. Whether building cutting-edge web solutions or diving into the intricate details of system optimization, Tommy's expertise is both broad and profound.

When not immersed in coding or writing, Tommy enjoys exploring the latest tech trends, tinkering with open-source projects, and mentoring aspiring developers. His enthusiasm for technology and dedication to empowering others shine through in everything he creates.

Join Tommy Clark on this exciting journey to unlock the full potential of technology—and get ready to be inspired, informed, and equipped to tackle your next big challenge!

Glossary: Go Programming for Beginners

A

Access Modifier: A keyword that determines the visibility of types, variables, and methods in Go. The primary access modifiers are public (exported) and private (unexported), determined by the case of the first letter of the identifier.

Array: A fixed-size collection of elements of the same type. Arrays have a defined length that cannotchange after their declaration.

B

Benchmark: A method to measure the performance of a section of code. In Go, benchmarking is doneusing the `testing` package and is especially useful for understanding the efficiency of algorithms.

C

Channel: A conduit that enables communication between goroutines. Channels are crucial for synchronizing operations and data exchange in concurrent programming.

Compiler: A tool that translates Go code (source code) into machine code that the computer can execute. The Go compiler performs various checks to ensure that the code is syntactically and semanticallycorrect.

Concurrency: The ability to run multiple tasks simultaneously in overlapping time periods. Go natively supports concurrent programming through goroutines and channels.

Goroutine: A lightweight thread managed by the Go runtime. Goroutines are used to achieveconcurrency and can be easily launched with the `go` keyword.

D

Deferred Function: A function call that is postponed until the surrounding function returns. The deferred function will execute in the reverse order of their declaration when the surrounding function isfinished.

E

Error Handling: The process of managing runtime errors in a program. In Go, errors are represented as a built-in interface type, and error handling is typically done by checking the returned error value.

F

Function: A block of code that performs a specific task and can return a value. Functions in Go are first-class citizens and can be passed around, returned from other functions, and assigned to variables.

For Loop: A control structure that allows repeated execution of a block of code as long as a specifiedcondition is true. Go provides a unique syntax for loops that can create both classic and 'while-style' loops.

G

Garbage Collection: The automated process of reclaiming memory that is no longer in use. Go has abuilt-in garbage collector that helps manage memory allocation and deallocation without manual intervention.

I

Interface: A type that specifies a contract of methods that a struct (or any other type) must implement. Interfaces support polymorphism, allowing different types to be treated as the same based on their methods.

M

Map: A built-in data structure in Go that associates keys with values. Maps provide fast lookups and can be used to store collections of data that require key-value relationships.

Module: A collection of related Go packages that are versioned together. Modules are used to manage dependencies and are defined in a `go.mod` file.

P

Pointer: A variable that holds the memory address of another variable. Pointers allow for efficient data manipulation without copying large structures.

Package: A collection of Go source files that are compiled together. Packages help organize code into reusable components and can be imported into other packages.

R

Receiver: A special variable that allows methods to be associated with a specific type. Receivers can be either value receivers (operating on a copy of the type) or pointer receivers (operating on the original instance).

S

Slice: A flexible, dynamically-sized view into an array. Unlike arrays, slices can grow and shrink, making them a more practical choice for managing collections of items in Go.

Struct: A composite data type that groups together variables (fields) under a single name. Structs are used to create complex data structures in Go.

Switch Statement: A control structure that allows for multi-way branching based on the value of an expression. It provides a cleaner alternative to a series of if-else statements.

T

Type Assertion: A mechanism to retrieve the dynamic type of an interface variable. Type assertions allow you to check whether an interface holds a specific type and retrieve its value.

Type Declaration: A statement that defines a new type based on an existing one. This can be used to create new types, enhancing clarity and intent in code.

V

Variable: A named storage location that can hold data of a specific type. Variables in Go must have a type declared, and can be initialized with a value when they are created.

www.ingramcontent.com/pod-product-compliance
Lightning Source LLC
LaVergne TN
LVHW051338050326
832903LV00031B/3604